W9-AZY-466

Korean War

Korean War
UPDATED EDITION

MAURICE ISSERMAN

JOHN S. BOWMAN
GENERAL EDITOR

Facts On File, Inc.

Facts On File, Inc.
132 West 31st Street
New York NY 10001

Library of Congress Cataloging-in-Publication Data
Isserman, Maurice.
Korean war : updated edition / by Maurice Isserman.
p. cm. — (America at war)
Rev. ed. of: The Korean War. 1992.
Includes bibliographical references and index.
ISBN 0-8160-4939-4
1. Korean War, 1950–1953—United States. 2. United States—Armed Forces—Korea (South)—History. 3. Korean War, 1950–1953. I. Title. II. Series.
DS919 .I77 2003
951.904'2373—dc21   2002007916

Facts On File books are available at special discounts when purchased in bulk quantities for businesses, associations, institutions, or sales promotions. Please call our Special Sales Department in New York at (212) 967-8800 or (800) 322-8755.

You can find Facts On File on the World Wide Web at http://www.factsonfile.com

Text design by Erika K. Arroyo
Logo design by Smart Graphics
Maps by Dale Williams

Printed in the United States of America

MP FOF 10 9 8 7 6 5 4 3 2 1

This book is printed on acid-free paper.

Note on Photos

Many of the illustrations and photographs used in this book are old, historical images. The quality of the prints is not always up to modern standards, as in some cases the originals are damaged. The content of the illustrations, however, made their inclusion important despite problems in reproduction.

Contents

Preface

The Korean War began in June 1950 and ended three years and one month later. Fifty-four thousand Americans died in the war, in addition to 1 million Chinese and perhaps 3.5 million Koreans. Despite this bloody record, the war is sometimes called America's forgotten war.

This book is an updated edition of *The Korean War,* originally published as part of the Facts On File America at War series in 1992. This edition offers many new features, including an expanded collection of photographs and maps and an updated and expanded list of recommended books at the end of the text. Readers will also find box features, brief articles or essays spaced throughout the narrative that discuss topics ranging from the role of Canadian forces in the war to a more current debate over alleged U.S. atrocities against Korean civilians. Finally, a glossary has been added, providing a quick reference to understand some of the more obscure and difficult terms that appear in the text.

Since the first edition of this book was published, Americans have been given repeated reminders that the Korean War does not deserve to be forgotten. One factor reminding Americans of the war's importance has been the passing of the generation of Americans who fought in Korea. Obituary columns in the nation's newspapers regularly feature reports of the death of the now-elderly veterans of the Korean War.

One such report ran in April 2002, in the *New York Times,* marking the death at age 82 of U.S. Marine Corps veteran William E. Barber. Barber was already a decorated combat veteran of World War II when the Korean War broke out in 1950. As a marine captain, he commanded Company F of the Second Battalion of the Seventh Marines, First Marine Division. He and his troops were part of the U.S. forces that spearheaded the counterattack against North Korea in the autumn of

1950. They were driving their way up the eastern side of North Korea toward the Yalu River that November when Chinese Communist forces launched an attack that turned back the American advance. In what became known as the Battle of the Chosin Reservoir—which is fully described in this volume—the marines made a legendary fighting retreat in the face of overwhelming odds. Captain Barber was in the thick of the battle.

At a critical moment in the marine withdrawal, Barber's company was assigned to hold a hill overlooking the Toktong Pass, a vital link on the road the Americans were taking to safety. Thousands of their fellow marines depended on Company F's ability to defend that hilltop. Under heavy Chinese attack, for five days and six nights, despite subzero weather and heavy snow and despite being wounded on the second day of the battle, Captain Barber kept his men fighting. "I knew that we could probably hold," he told a reporter after the war, "and I knew that if we didn't hold we could exact a very heavy toll." Hector Cafferata, one of the riflemen under his command, recalled that Barber ignored his wound and refused to be treated as an invalid; instead, "he walked the line, he kept us together." In the end, 82 of Company F's original 240 men were left unscathed; they had killed more than 1,000 of the enemy. Captain Barber was awarded a Congressional Medal of Honor for his role in the defense of the hilltop. "He was one tough guy," Private Cafferata recalled, something that Cafferata would know about—he won his own Medal of Honor for valor displayed in the same engagement.

Aside from recognizing the courage and sacrifices made by so many Americans in the Korean War, such an obituary should serve to remind 21st-century youth that, as remote as it may seem in time and space, this war is still a very real event to many of their elders. In fact, while still overshadowed in popular memory by World War II and the Vietnam War, the Korean War became measurably less "forgotten" in the United States in the course of the 1990s. One important milestone in remembering the war took place on July 27, 1995, the 42nd anniversary of the signing of the armistice that ended the war, when the Korean War Veterans Memorial was dedicated in Washington, D.C., to the memory of the 1.75 million U.S. servicemen and women who took part in the conflict. Sitting on 2.2 acres adjacent to the Lincoln Memorial Reflecting Pool, the memorial consists of a group of 19 statues representing a column of U.S. combat foot soldiers in helmets and ponchos moving outward toward an American flag. U.S. president Bill Clinton and South

PREFACE

Korean president Kim Dae Jung took part in the opening ceremonies. President Clinton told the audience, which included many veterans and their families, that the "free world's participation in the Korean War, its first resolute and effective action to stem the expansion of Communism, changed the course of history. In this sense, I would say that the Korean War was the war that heralded the collapse of the Berlin Wall and the demise of Communism."

Historians also looked back to the war in the 1990s. Among the consequences of the "demise of Communism" was the sudden availability of new historical sources on the Korean War from the Communist side, as Soviet presidential and foreign ministry archives in Moscow were opened up for the first time to the scrutiny of Western historians. According to Kathryn Weathersby, one of the historians most familiar with these new sources, the Moscow archives "reveal a great deal more than has previously been known about the relationship between the Soviet Union and North Korea, the decision-making surrounding the attack on South Korea, the role of Mao Zedong (Mao Tse-tung) in all stages of the war, the formulation of the Communist positions at the armistice negotiations, and the role of Stalin's death in bringing the war to an end."

History is a work in progress. Historians are always coming up with new sources and new interpretations to guide their understanding of the past. This has certainly been true in the case of the Korean War since the 1990s. Sergei Goncharov, John W. Lewis, and Xue Litai wrote one of the first of the new wave of books on the Korean War to be based on Moscow's diplomatic archives. In *Uncertain Partners: Stalin, Mao, and the Korean War* (1993), the three historians (one each from Russia, the United States, and China) concluded that the new sources proved conclusively that the North Korean invasion of South Korea in June 1950 "was preplanned, blessed, and directly assisted by Stalin and his generals, and reluctantly backed by Mao at Stalin's insistence." Other historians, in contrast, examining the same sources, have emphasized Stalin's reluctance to approve Kim Il Sung's plans for invading the South and his desire to minimize the Soviet role once war did break out. Kathryn Weathersby wrote in 1995 in the bulletin of the Washington-based Cold War International History Project that the Soviet documents "show that the initiative for the North Korean attack on South Korea on 25 June 1950 was clearly Kim Il Sung's. Kim requested Stalin's approval several times in 1949 before the Soviet leader finally agreed in early 1950 to support a North Korean offensive." Of the three Communist leaders involved in the decisions that led to the war, Stalin, Mao, and Kim, only Kim—the least important of the three—seemed to have no doubts that the invasion was a gamble worth taking. As John Lewis Gaddis showed in *We Now Know: Rethinking Cold War History* (1997), Kim shuttled back and forth between Moscow and Beijing in the months before the invasion, coaxing and wheedling Stalin and Mao, reporting to each one separately that the other was a strong proponent of invasion, and "thereby achieving the feat of having exaggerated to both the Russians and the Chinese the degree to which each supported what he himself wanted to do." Here was truly a case of the tail wagging the dog.

In 1995 President Clinton spoke of the war as a notable early victory in the long struggle of the United States to contain communism. It is certainly true that the United States emerged at the end of the Korean War with a much more powerful military establishment than it had possessed in 1950 and with a much greater willingness to use that power wherever and whenever it perceived a threat of expanding Soviet influence. Many historians agree that the war proved a setback to the Soviet Union; Stalin's successors knew better than to ever again launch a direct and open assault on an American ally. "Of the great powers," William Stueck concluded in his well-regarded book *The Korean War: An International History* (1995), "the Soviet Union clearly was the prime loser by virtue of the Korean War."

But Stueck and other historians are less inclined to see the war as an unambiguous victory for the West in the cold war. If the Soviets fared poorly, that was not the case of the other emerging communist superpower—China. The Korean War, Stueck argued, "contributed enormously to the international prestige of the new China, which fought the world's greatest power to a standstill." U.S. policy makers would remember the impact of Chinese intervention in the Korean War, and that memory would prove a decisive factor in constraining the application of U.S. military force in its next major armed conflict, in Vietnam, a dozen years later.

The Korean War left an ambiguous legacy, not least because the issues left undecided at its conclusion continue to trouble the world a half-century later. When the war ended in 1953, the communist government that ruled the northern half of the Korean Peninsula—the Democratic Republic of North Korea, as it styled itself—was an absolute dictatorship, headed by its ruthless founder Kim Il Sung. Kim

PREFACE

would remain in power in Pyongyang, North Korea's capital city, for an additional 41 years, until his death in 1994—long outliving his principal communist allies, Joseph Stalin of the Soviet Union and Mao Zedong of the People's Republic of China, as well as his principal anticommunist adversaries, Syngman Rhee of South Korea and Harry S. Truman of the United States. Kim would come to enjoy the historical distinction of being the only international leader to remain alive and in power throughout the entire era of the cold war.

In the meantime, of course, much of the rest of the world had changed dramatically. The cold war came to an end in 1989 with the fall of the Berlin Wall. Communism in the Soviet Union—and, for that matter, the Soviet Union itself—came to an end in 1991. The People's Republic of China would survive the 1990s and remain under the absolute rule of the Chinese Communist Party, but long before the end of the 20th century the Chinese economy had come to bear a distinct resemblance to the capitalist economies of the West. At the start of the 21st century, there remained only a few bastions of the once seemingly mighty communist system, and none of those presented a significant ideological challenge either to their neighbors or to the world's one remaining superpower, the United States.

The world changed dramatically between the 1950s and the 1990s, but North Korea did not. The country remained a grim and isolated example of all that was worst in the history of communism, representing a kind of museum piece of Stalinist misrule in its repressive totalitarian regime, its economic stagnation, and its bristling hostility to the surrounding world. Again, anyone who thinks that Korea is far removed from current concerns is not paying close attention to the news these days, news that this volume helps to place in a meaningful context.

Kim Il Sung's death in 1994 initially raised hopes, particularly in neighboring South Korea, that the next generation of North Korean leaders would be willing to abandon old hostilities and embrace change. Kim's successor as leader of North Korea, his son Kim Jong Il (Kim Chong Il), did, in fact, make occasional gestures toward internal reform and reconciliation with the South. He allowed some South Koreans to enjoy family reunions in the North with relatives they had not seen since the Korean War. He permitted some sports and cultural exchanges between the two Koreas. And he allowed some South Korean tourists to visit the North. He also made some gestures of reconciliation toward the United States. There were tentative diplomatic contacts between the two countries, and North Korea handed over the remains of some U.S. military personnel who had been missing in action since the Korean War.

But such gestures did not change North Korea's status as an international pariah. Although North Korea was desperately poor, with widespread starvation reported in the countryside, North Korean leaders devoted at least 25 percent of their economy's annual gross national product to military expenditures. North Korea's 1 million active-duty soldiers, along with hundreds of thousands of airmen and sailors, represented the fifth largest active-duty military force in the world in the 1990s. Neighboring countries in Asia, as well as the United States, watched warily as the regime began to develop a ballistic missile system in the mid-1990s, capable of delivering conventional (and perhaps in time, nuclear) warheads to targets hundreds of miles away. In one notorious test, a North Korean missile barreled provocatively through Japanese air space. In the face of international outcry, North Korea suspended further test flights but continued to stockpile missiles.

With the end of the cold war, many of the battlefields from that conflict began to attract hordes of the reverent and the curious. Like the tourists who regularly visit Civil War battlefields at Gettysburg National Military Park or World War II battlefields on the Normandy beaches, Americans could be found visiting places such as Khe Sanh and the Ia Drang Valley in Vietnam. But there were no tourists to be found visiting the heavily militarized 38th parallel, which divides the two Koreas. Instead, there were 37,000 American soldiers on a high state of combat readiness who continued to patrol the border between the two Koreas. According to U.S. Army general Thomas A. Schwartz, commander of U.S. forces in Korea, at any given moment, "70 percent of the Army is either getting ready to go in, is in Korea, or just came out of Korea." In the event of a renewed North Korean assault on South Korea, there is no question that the United States would quickly and massively intervene in the conflict.

Captain Barber never got to revisit the hilltop where he earned his Medal of Honor. It will likely be some years before American tourists can walk the battlefields of the Chosin Reservoir or shop for souvenirs in a Pyongyang flea market. The Korean War is all too much still with people today—which is all the more reason why it is a war that should not be forgotten.

1

TASK FORCE SMITH

On the evening of June 30, 1950, unexpected and unwelcome news reached a few hundred soldiers of the U.S. Army's Twenty-fourth Infantry Division stationed in Japan. They were told to get their gear together immediately. They were leaving for South Korea. They were going to be the first U.S. soldiers to fight in the Korean War.

Five days earlier, on June 25, soldiers from communist North Korea (known as the North Korean People's Army, or NKPA) had launched an invasion of their noncommunist neighbor, South Korea. South Korean troops (known as Republic of Korea, or ROK, forces) were surprised, outnumbered, and outgunned by the invaders. Though some South Koreans fought bravely, many others fled in terror from the communists. In the first week of the war, ROK forces suffered 44,000 casualties—killed, wounded, captured or missing—just under half their total strength. Unless something was done quickly, all of South Korea would fall to the invaders.

On June 27, President Harry S. Truman ordered U.S. military forces based in Japan to launch air and naval strikes against the North Korean invaders in the South. Later that same day the United Nations (UN) Security Council, meeting in New York, voted in support of a resolution calling upon member nations to defend South Korea against North Korean aggression. On June 28, U.S. bombers and fighters went into action over the Korean Peninsula. Gen. Douglas MacArthur, commander of the U.S. Far East Command based in Japan, was given overall

NORTHWEST PACIFIC, 1950

USSR

MONGOLIA

Sea of
Japan

NORTH KOREA

SOUTH KOREA

PACIFIC
OCEAN

Yellow
Sea

CHINA

JAPAN

East
China
Sea

KOREAN PENINSULA

CHINA

Najin

NORTH
KOREA

Sinuiju   Hamhung

TAIWAN

Sunchon
Wonsan

Sea of
Japan

Chinnampo   Pyongyang

THAI-
LAND

South
China
Sea

PHILIPPINES

Kaesong

SOUTH
Seoul KOREA

Inchon

FRENCH
INDOCHINA

Yellow
Sea

Suwon   Wonju

Chongju

Taejon Pohang

Kunsan   Taegu

Chonju

Chinju   Masan

N

Kwangju

Pusan

0   500 miles

0   500 km

Cheju

control of UN efforts to aid South Korea. Stretching the limits of his
orders from Washington, MacArthur ordered U.S. planes to hit targets
north of the 38th parallel, which divided North and South Korea, as well
as the invading NKPA forces in the South.

TASK FORCE SMITH

In response to the invasion of South Korea by the North Korean army, President Harry S. Truman (1884–1972) declares a state of national emergency on June 27, 1950. *(National Archives)*

Meanwhile, the Joint Chiefs of Staff of the U.S. military services, meeting in Washington, authorized MacArthur to send U.S. ground forces to South Korea if he thought it necessary. The following day, June 29, MacArthur flew to South Korea for a quick inspection tour. He saw Seoul, the South Korean capital, in flames and about to fall to the communists. ROK forces were retreating in panic, throwing away their weapons and uniforms. When MacArthur returned to Japan later that day he cabled Washington, advising an all-out American military effort, including the use of air, naval, and ground forces. Otherwise, he warned, the defense of South Korea would be "doomed to failure."

Just before midnight on June 29, Washington time, MacArthur's cable arrived at the Pentagon, requesting the dispatch of two U.S. Army divisions to South Korea. Aides awakened President Truman at about 5 A.M. next morning with the news. Truman ordered MacArthur to get a regimental combat team of a few thousand U.S. soldiers into combat in South Korea as soon as possible; later that morning he approved orders for tens of thousands more to follow them.

Douglas A. MacArthur
(1880–1964), General
of the Armies, U.S.A.
(National Archives)

Even getting a few thousand troops together to fight in South Korea was no easy matter. MacArthur had four army divisions (about 50,000 men) under his command in Japan. These occupation garrisons were the nearest U.S. forces available. But they were far from combat-ready. Occupation duty in Japan was known in the postwar military as a very soft assignment. With the Japanese economy still recovering from the devastation of World War II, even enlisted men in the U.S. Army could live very comfortably there. Many enjoyed the attentions of Japanese servants and girlfriends. As a fighting force, U.S. soldiers in Japan were undertrained, poorly disciplined, and poorly equipped. And there were neither plans nor the necessary planes and ships to get them to the battlefront in a hurry.

While he mobilized his forces, MacArthur ordered a token force of Americans to leave immediately for South Korea. The U.S. military command in Japan believed that the sight of American soldiers at the front would improve the morale and stiffen the resistance of their South Korean allies. No one in MacArthur's headquarters, or in Washington, respected the fighting qualities of the communist North Koreans. They referred to them as *gooks*—a racially insulting term. Surely when the North Koreans realized they were up against the overwhelming power of the United States of America, they would turn around and flee back to the North.

Two companies of the First Battalion, Twenty-first Infantry Regiment, Twenty-fourth Infantry Division, based on the Japanese island of Kyushu, were ordered to Korea on June 30. They were nicknamed Task Force Smith, after their commanding officer, Lt. Col. Charles "Brad" Smith, a 34-year-old West Point graduate and veteran of the Guadalcanal campaign in the Pacific in World War II. Smith's men faced a long, tiring trip from their barracks in Japan to the front line in Korea. Leaving their barracks at 3 A.M. on July 1, they embarked on a five-hour truck ride through heavy rain to the airfield at Itasuki. There they boarded U.S. Air Force C-54 transport planes, which carried them across the Sea of Japan to an airstrip near Korea's southern port city of Pusan. They stepped off the planes and onto Korean soil at 11 A.M. on July 1.

For most of the men of Task Force Smith, Korea would be their introduction to combat. Some of them were cooks and clerks who had not been trained as infantrymen. The average age of the enlisted men in the unit was 20, too young to have fought in World War II, which had ended just five years earlier. On July 2, the Americans boarded railroad flatcars in Pusan that would carry them northward. As they waited to pull out, a train arrived, filled with refugees and soldiers just back from the front. The sight of the train provided one of Task Force Smith's officers, 1st Lt. Philip Day, Jr., with his first inkling of the disasters of war that the Americans were to encounter. The train

> was covered with human beings—troops, officers, old men, women, children and most important, at least to me, wounded. My God, I thought, maybe there was a real war going on!

Worse sights awaited them the farther north they traveled. As the train carrying Task Force Smith reached the town of Pyongtaek, it passed the wreckage of another South Korean train, bombed mistakenly by UN pilots who thought they were over North Korean–

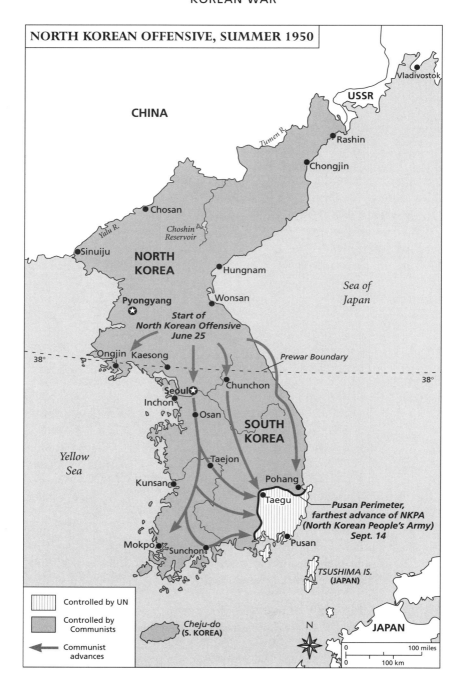

NORTH KOREAN OFFENSIVE, SUMMER 1950

Vladivostok

USSR

CHINA

Tumen R.

Rashin

Chongjin

Chosan

*Choshin
Reservoir*

Yalu R.

Sinuiju

**NORTH
KOREA**

Hungnam

*Sea of
Japan*

Pyongyang

Wonsan

*Start of
North Korean Offensive
June 25*

38°

Ongjin   Kaesong

Prewar Boundary

38°

Chunchon

Seoul

Inchon

Osan

**SOUTH
KOREA**

*Yellow
Sea*

Taejon

Pohang

Kunsan

Taegu

*Pusan Perimeter,
farthest advance of NKPA
(North Korean People's Army)
Sept. 14*

Mokpo

Sunchon

Pusan

*TSUSHIMA IS.
(JAPAN)*

Controlled by UN

Controlled by
Communists

Communist
advances

Cheju-do
(S. KOREA)

N

JAPAN

0   100 miles

0   100 km

controlled territory. The corpses of hundreds of dead ROK soldiers and South Korean civilians lay strewn around. When the Americans got off the train and climbed into trucks heading north, they found the roads clogged with refugees and ROK soldiers desperately fleeing the communist advance. Nevertheless, the young American soldiers and their officers remained confident that once they reached the front they would turn the tide of battle.

U.S. military commanders in Korea ordered Task Force Smith to block the path of the onrushing North Korean soldiers. Seoul, the capital of South Korea, had already fallen to the Communists, who were now heading southward along the Seoul-Pusan highway. The Americans would take up positions on a stretch of the highway about 50 miles south of Seoul, between the towns of Suwon and Osan. Lieutenant Colonel Smith had driven up ahead of his troops in a jeep to reconnoiter the area. Task Force Smith, reinforced by 108 artillerymen from the Fifty-second Field Artillery Battalion and six other 105 mm howitzers, followed their colonel northward by truck.

Smith picked out what he thought would be a good defensive position on three hills that overlooked the main road. His men arrived about 3 A.M. on July 5, their clothes soaked through from a cold drizzle. They moved into the hills to dig foxholes and dragged heavy boxes of ammunition up through the mud to their positions. "Everyone was tired, wet, cold, and a little bit pissed off," Lieutenant Day would recall. The overcast skies also meant that the soldiers of Task Force Smith could expect no help from the U.S. Air Force if they got into trouble.

Trouble was not long in coming. Shortly after dawn a sergeant called Day's attention to a column of tanks moving down the road. Lieutenant Day, excited and unsure of what he was seeing, asked what they were. The sergeant replied calmly, "Those are T-34 tanks, sir, and I don't think they're going to be friendly toward us."

The artillerymen, who had set up their howitzers about a mile south of Smith's infantrymen, zeroed in on the tanks. They fired the first American shots of the ground war in Korea at 8:16 A.M. on July 5, 1950. The infantrymen opened up with their 75 mm recoilless rifles, bazookas, and mortars. Although four North Korean tanks were knocked out, many of the American shells, left over from World War II, turned out to be duds. The Americans began to take casualties in return. One North Korean crewman, abandoning his wrecked tank, fired his machine gun at Americans as he leapt to the ground. An American

Infantry skirmish line lays down a base of fire. *(Lyndon Baines Johnson Library & Museum)*

machine gunner fell dead before the enemy tankman was killed. The name of the dead American, the first U.S. death of the war, has been lost to history. Lieutenant Day, firing on the tanks with a 75 mm recoilless rifle, found himself a target of North Korean tank fire; his gun was destroyed and the concussion caused blood to pour from his ears. All the while the North Korean tanks kept rolling south. Within two hours after the fighting started, 29 tanks had passed by Task Force Smith, and 20 Americans had been killed or wounded.

An hour later trucks carrying thousands of North Korean infantrymen rolled down the highway to the American positions. U.S. artillery fire blew up several trucks, killing dozens of NKPA soldiers. The rest climbed out of their trucks and began to encircle the Americans. Colonel Smith pulled his forces together into a tighter perimeter, and they fought back with rifles, grenades, and artillery. Many on both sides were killed.

Finally, Colonel Smith was left with no choice but to withdraw or risk the destruction of his entire unit. The Americans had to abandon their wounded to the enemy. Some of the young soldiers panicked, throwing away their weapons so that they could travel faster. Lieutenant

Day recalled: "We moved as fast as we could. Everything had broken down and it was every man for himself." Colonel Smith and some of his men were able to break out of the enemy encirclement, but when the battle was done, more than 185 Americans had been killed, wounded, captured, or were missing.

News of the destruction of Task Force Smith spread quickly through the ranks of American soldiers arriving in South Korea, undermining their morale. Things had not worked out the way the planners in Tokyo and Washington thought they would. All in all, it was an unpromising beginning for the first full-scale American war on the Asian mainland, a conflict that Gen. Omar N. Bradley, chairman of the U.S. Joint Chiefs of Staff, would in the spring of 1951 call the "wrong war in the wrong place at the wrong time."

Task Force Smith never really had a chance. The unit was in part the victim of an arrogant miscalculation by U.S. military commanders, a presumption that the North Koreans would never stand and fight against Americans. But the soldiers of Task Force Smith were also

U.S. truck convoy crossing the Naktong River passes a knocked-out T-34 tank, made in USSR. *(U.S. Army Military History Institute)*

victims of the uncertainty and confusion in American foreign policy in Asia since the end of the World War II. Between 1945 and 1950, the U.S. government committed itself to the struggle to stop communism wherever it threatened to spread—a struggle that became known as the cold war. Yet neither the leaders of the American government nor the American people as a whole seemed to realize, or were willing to pay, the true costs of a policy of anticommunist "containment" on a worldwide scale. The U.S. government and military had spent five years getting ready to fight a World War II–style conflict on the European continent. That would have been the "right" war, in terms of American expectations and preparation. A limited war in Asia was another matter altogether.

Yet the Korean War would mark a dividing line in American history. It was the moment when the U.S. truly became a superpower, displaying the will and developing the means for global intervention.

With the end of World War II in 1945, the wartime Grand Alliance of the United States and the Soviet Union against Nazi Germany collapsed. President Franklin Roosevelt had hoped that the United States and the Soviets could cooperate in guaranteeing the peace and stability of the postwar international order. But when Soviet leader Joseph Stalin imposed a system of puppet communist regimes on the countries of Eastern and central Europe, the bright hopes of postwar friendship faded. The United States strengthened the defenses of Western Europe against further Soviet advances. George Kennan, an American foreign service officer in the U.S. embassy in Moscow, sent a long telegram to the State Department in February 1946, analyzing postwar Soviet policies. In an expanded version of his telegram, printed in the influential journal *Foreign Affairs* in 1947, Kennan warned of the hostility of the Soviet leadership to the Western world and their determination to spread the communist system beyond its present borders. In what became known as the "containment doctrine," Kennan declared:

> In these circumstances, it is clear that the main element of any United States policy toward the Soviet Union must be that of a long-term, patient but firm and vigilant containment of Russian expansive tendencies.

President Harry Truman agreed with Kennan. (Truman had been Franklin Roosevelt's vice president and had become president after Roosevelt's death in April 1945.) On March 12, 1947, he made a speech

Japan

FORWARD BASE FOR THE U.S. WAR EFFORT

AMONG THE CRUCIAL FACTORS THAT ALLOWED THE United States to halt the North Korean advance in the summer of 1950 was the fact that the Japanese port of Sasebo was only 165 nautical miles away from the South Korean port of Pusan. Since Japan's surrender and occupation in September 1945, the United States had maintained an extensive series of military bases in the country. American occupation troops and supplies already located in Japan could thus be rushed by ship or plane to Korea in the crucial days and weeks following the North Korean invasion. Japan served as headquarters for the UN Command, under Gen. Douglas MacArthur, and throughout the war functioned as an advanced staging base for the U.S. military. Wounded UN servicemen were sent to military hospitals in Japan. Although the Japanese were not permitted to maintain their own armed forces and took no direct role in the fighting, Japanese guards at U.S. military installations freed up U.S. soldiers for fighting in Korea, while Japanese sailors were recruited to operate minesweepers and landing craft in Korean waters.

to Congress calling for the extension of U.S. economic and military aid to Greece and Turkey, to aid their resistance to communism. Truman told Congress, in what became known as the Truman Doctrine, that it "must be the policy of the United States to support free peoples who are resisting subjugation by armed minorities or by outside pressures." Congress approved aid to Greece and Turkey and also voted for the Marshall Plan, an ambitious foreign aid program providing funds to help rebuild the war-shattered economies of Western Europe. And in 1949 the Senate ratified a treaty establishing the North Atlantic Treaty Organization (NATO), committing the United States to the continued military defense of Western Europe.

Yet the old isolationist habits that had shaped American policy since the earliest days of the republic were far from dead and buried in the late 1940s. Many Americans still wanted to isolate their country from "foreign entanglements," as George Washington had advised. The open-ended pledge to defend the "free world" against communism was more rhetorical than real. Sheltered between two great oceans, Americans were used to staying out of foreign wars; once forced to fight, they preferred to disband and disarm their armies as quickly as possible when the guns were silent. The aftermath of World War II was no exception. U.S. military forces shrank from 12 million men in 1945 to just 1.6 million in 1947. Annual military spending over the same period shrank from $82 billion to $13 billion. These cutbacks still left the U.S. military a much more powerful force than it had been on the eve of the World War II. And U.S. government leaders hoped that their monopoly on the atomic bomb, which had been used with decisive effect against the Japanese cities of Hiroshima and Nagasaki in 1945, would ensure American power.

Although the United States maintained major bases in Japan, Hawaii, and the Philippines, the great bulk of U.S. military forces overseas were stationed in Europe. Yet it was in Asia that the Communists were making some of their greatest advances in the years after World War II. In Vietnam, a French colony, a guerrilla war led by the Communist Ho Chi Minh challenged the continued rule of the colonialists. At the same time in China, Communist armies led by Mao Zedong were on the verge of overthrowing the government of the country's anticommunist leader, Chiang Kai-shek (Jiang Jeshi). The Truman administration left the fighting in Vietnam for the moment to the French. In China the United States provided several billion dollars' worth of military aid to Chiang Kai-shek but carefully avoided any direct involvement of U.S. military forces. While some Americans felt strongly that the United States should be doing more to defeat the communists in Asia, neither the Democratic president Harry Truman, nor his Republican critics in Congress, showed any enthusiasm for raising taxes to pay for greater military spending.

In 1949, two events shook Americans' self-confidence in their ability to triumph in the cold war: The Chinese Communists defeated Chiang Kai-shek's forces, driving them from the mainland into exile on the large offshore island of Taiwan, and the Soviet Union exploded its own atomic bomb. Early in 1950 President Truman authorized officials from the State and Defense Departments to study the threat to American interests in the world. The result was a top-secret study known as NSC-68 (NSC means National Security Council, the government body that advises the president on foreign policy issues). It warned that American credibility in world affairs had been seriously shaken by the fall of China and the end of the U.S. monopoly on the atomic bomb. No more setbacks could be allowed in any corner of the globe because "the assault on free institutions is worldwide now, and . . . a defeat of free institutions anywhere is a defeat everywhere."

The United States had thought about the Soviet-American conflict chiefly in terms of an all-out war with the Soviet Union, a war centered on the European continent. But it had to prepare to fight limited wars in many other parts of the world. To make this strategy possible, NSC-68 called for a tripling of the defense budget to finance a vast expansion of American nuclear and conventional forces. In May 1950, in line with the recommendations of NSC-68, Truman extended U.S. military aid to the French war effort in Vietnam. But it was by no means certain that proposals for such a huge increase in defense spending could get through a budget-conscious Congress.

The Korean War changed all that. When North Korean forces attacked in June 1950, American policy makers believed the war signaled the start of a full-scale war with the Soviet Union and its allies. Margaret Truman, the president's daughter, was with him in their home in Independence, Missouri, when he received the news of the invasion. "My father made it clear," she recalled, "from the moment he heard the news, that he feared this was the opening round in World War Three." By August, according to public opinion polls, a majority of Americans agreed that the fighting in Korea was in fact the start of a third world war. Over the next three years, while Americans fought, bled, and died in Korea, the United States rearmed and reshaped its foreign policy. For the men of Task Force Smith and thousands of others flung into combat into Korea in the next few months, the renewed emphasis on American military preparedness came too late.

2
BACKGROUND TO WAR

Today there are two Koreas: the Republic of Korea (ROK, or South Korea) and the Democratic People's Republic of Korea (DPRK, or North Korea). For more than 1,000 years before the 20th century, Korea was one undivided country. The present border shared by the two Koreas runs through the middle of the Korean Peninsula. The border dips to the south of the 38th parallel along its western edge and rises slightly to the north of the 38th parallel as it moves eastward from the town of Panmunjom. It was in Panmunjom that an agreement was reached in 1953 ending the Korean War after three bloody years of fighting. The cease-fire line, which marked the positions held by the two opposing sides, became the border between North and South Korea. Heavily armed soldiers have kept careful watch along both sides of that border ever since 1953, a constant reminder that this is a political, not a geographic, boundary line.

Much of Korea's history, for better or worse, has been shaped by the country's geographic location. The Korean Peninsula juts southward about 600 miles from the Asian mainland, dividing the Sea of Japan on its eastern shore from the shallow Yellow Sea on its western shore. The peninsula is a small area of about 85,000 square miles, or roughly the same size as Minnesota. At its widest, the peninsula is less than 200 miles across, and at its narrowest it is less than 100 miles across. A number of small islands lie off its shores.

The interior of the Korean Peninsula consists mainly of rugged hills and mountains. Mountains run the length of the peninsula, with the highest peak more than 9,000 feet in elevation. The Taebaek Mountains cut off a large part of the eastern coast from the western half of the peninsula. Because of the barren mountain terrain, most human settlement and agricultural cultivation is restricted to the river valleys and coastal plains, which make up a fifth of the peninsula's land area. Korea's climate is harsh: Long, cold winters are followed by hot and humid summers. The soil is poor, except in the intensively fertilized rice paddies or in fields where farmers grow wheat, millet, barley, and some cotton. The northern half of the peninsula has some natural resources to offer, including deposits of coal and iron ore.

Koreans are an ancient people. The modern inhabitants of Korea are descendants of migrants from Manchuria and Mongolia who traveled southward in about 3000 B.C. Historians disagree as to the beginning of Korea as a separate country, but some date its origins to 1123 B.C., when a Chinese prince named Chi-tzu came from China with 5,000 followers and established his rule in a kingdom located in the area of present-day Pyongyang, the capital of North Korea. Known in ancient times as Choson (or "Land of the Morning Calm"), Korea was divided into warring kingdoms until the seventh century A.D. A politically unified state first emerged in A.D. 676 under a kingdom known as Silla. In A.D. 935 another of the warring kingdoms of earlier centuries, known as Koguryo, or Koryo, gained control of the peninsula. It was from *Koryo* that the English word *Korea* was derived.

Korean independence proved precarious, since the country lies so near the great powers of East Asia. On its northern border, Korea is separated from Manchuria (China's northeastern province) by the Yalu River. Russia (known from 1917 to 1991 as the Soviet Union) shares a small stretch of Korea's northern border. The northern tip of Korea is only 90 miles south from the Russian port of Vladivostok. To the east, a short sea journey of 120 miles separates southern Korea from Japan. As a result the Korean Peninsula has acted, historically, as a natural land bridge between the powers of the Asian mainland and the Japanese.

Through much of Korea's history, China was the dominant power in the region. The Korean language, economy, political system, and religion (a mixture of Buddhism and Confucianism) bear the imprint of Chinese influence. The Chinese sometimes ruled Korea directly, other times indirectly. They regarded the Koreans as a "younger brother." But throughout 1,000 years of Chinese influence, the Koreans maintained a sense of their own separate national identity. When they had any say in

Officers and crew of the USS *Monocacy* stand on deck, Korea, June 1871. *(National Archives/DOD, War & Conflict, #0267)*

the matter, Koreans shunned contact with foreigners. The country became known as the "hermit kingdom" for its isolation.

Koreans could not maintain their isolation in the face of pressures from more powerful neighbors. The Mongols invaded the country in the 13th century, and the Japanese in the 16th century. In the 19th century, merchants and missionaries from Western countries began to appear, though the Koreans at first would have nothing to do with them. When a U.S. merchant ship put in to the Taedong River near Pyongyang in 1866, seeking to open trade with the Koreans, the local population massacred its crew. In 1871, in a belated act of retaliation, a U.S. naval squadron bombarded the forts guarding the entrance to the Han River. The Japanese were the most persistent of those seeking entry into Korea, forcing Koreans to open ports to their merchants in the 1870s. To counter the growing Japanese influence, Korea signed a series of treaties opening trade with Western powers, including one with the United States in 1882.

In the late 19th century the Japanese were beginning to develop a powerful and far-flung empire, extending their influence into Taiwan (a large island off the shore of southeast China), into southern Manchuria, and into Korea. China was a weak and divided country at this time and was easily defeated by Japan in the Sino-Japanese War of 1894–95, a war fought in part over the question of which country would control Korea. The Japanese government sent troops to occupy Seoul in 1894 to protect Japanese interests. Japan then bested its remaining military rival in the region, czarist Russia, in a war in 1905. The growth of Japanese power spelled doom for Korea's independence. In 1909 a high Japanese official in Korea was assassinated by a Korean nationalist; in response the Japanese annexed the country in 1910.

For the next 35 years Korea was ruled from Tokyo. The Japanese looked down on the Koreans and treated them harshly. Although Korea benefited from the roads, railroads, ports, and dams built by the Japanese, most of the profits were carried off to Japan. The Japanese seized land from Korean peasants and used the country as a source of raw materials, cheap labor, and conscript soldiers. When students launched an independence movement on March 1, 1919, Japanese authorities responded with a bloody crackdown, killing close to 7,000 people and

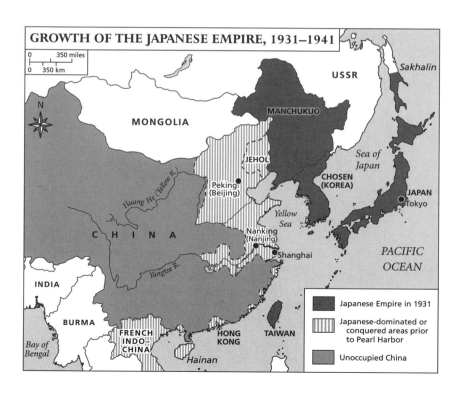

GROWTH OF THE JAPANESE EMPIRE, 1931–1941

0   350 miles
0   350 km

N

MONGOLIA

USSR

Sakhalin

MANCHUKUO

JEHOL

Sea of Japan

CHOSEN (KOREA)

Peking (Beijing)

Huang He (Yellow R.)

Yellow Sea

JAPAN
Tokyo

C H I N A

Nanking (Nanjing)

Shanghai

Yangtze R.

PACIFIC OCEAN

INDIA

BURMA

FRENCH INDO-CHINA

HONG KONG

TAIWAN

Bay of Bengal

Hainan

Japanese Empire in 1931

Japanese-dominated or conquered areas prior to Pearl Harbor

Unoccupied China

arresting thousands more. In memory of those events, March 1 is still observed in South Korea as Independence Movement Day. Some Koreans collaborated with their Japanese rulers; Korean members of the Japanese-organized national police force were especially feared and hated by other Koreans for their brutality.

Koreans never lost hope that they would one day regain their independence. Opposition movements soon sprang up against Japanese rule. One was led by a man named Syngman Rhee. Rhee was born in 1875, the son of a Korean scholar. He was thrown in jail for antigovernment activities in 1898. Following his release from prison in 1904, Rhee went to the United States, where he studied at Princeton University, receiving a Ph.D. in international law. A convert to Christianity, Rhee returned to Korea in 1910 to work for the Christian Youth movement. Suspected by the Japanese of pro-independence activities, Rhee escaped from Korea before he could be arrested. He would not return for more than three decades. At a meeting of Korean exiles in Shanghai in 1919, a Korean Provisional Government was established, with Rhee as its president. Rhee's "government" had no real power, and Rhee continued to have many rivals among Korean exiles for leadership of the independence movement. Many Korean nationalists disliked Rhee for his arrogance and distrusted his personal ambitions. But Rhee enjoyed the support of influential American backers, particularly Christian missionaries. Through all his long years of exile, he worked ceaselessly to win the backing of the U.S. government for an independent Korea under his leadership.

The Communists proved to be Rhee's most dangerous rivals in the Korean independence movement. In 1917, communists had launched a successful revolution in Russia. They called for a world revolution against capitalism and colonialism and found followers in many countries. China developed its own powerful communist movement in the 1920s and 1930s. Many Koreans lived in Siberia and in Manchuria. Some, swept up in the Russian and Chinese revolutions, became communists. Communists inside Korea risked torture and execution at the hands of the Japanese if they were captured. In Manchuria, Korean communists fought alongside Chinese Communists in the guerrilla war against the Japanese, who had set up a puppet regime there in the early 1930s.

One of the Communist leaders who emerged from the Manchurian fighting was a man known as Kim Il Sung. Few details are known about his early life. He was born in a peasant family near the city of Pyongyang in 1912. He attended school in Manchuria, where he joined the communist movement, and began fighting with the guerrillas in 1932. In 1941 he moved to Khabarovsk in the Soviet Far East, where he and his men joined the Soviet Red Army. His activities and whereabouts during the World War II are unknown, but at the end of the war he was with the Soviets as they prepared to attack the Japanese. North Korean propaganda would later invent unlikely tales of Kim's glorious deeds in the anti-Japanese struggle, but there is no question that he was a hardened and experienced guerrilla fighter.

When Americans remember World War II in the Pacific, they usually think in terms of the "island-hopping" campaigns (Guadalcanal, Tarawa, Iwo Jima, Okinawa) and the great naval battles (Midway, Coral Sea, Leyte Gulf). But there was another part of the war that the United States had little to do with. Throughout the war, much of the Japanese army was tied down in the battle for control of China. As U.S. military planners prepared to invade the Japanese home islands in the last stage of the war, they feared that this huge reserve force could be brought home to resist the Americans. It was expected that hundreds of thousands of U.S. soldiers and marines would lose their lives in the invasion of Japan, if the Japanese continued to resist to the last man, as they had on many Pacific islands. So U.S. strategists, including the U.S. military commander in the Pacific, Gen. Douglas MacArthur, were eager to draw the Soviet Union into the war. If the Red Army could sweep down from Siberia into Manchuria and engage the Japanese forces there, the U.S. invasion of Japan would be less costly. At a meeting of Allied leaders in the Soviet city of Yalta in February 1945, Soviet leader Joseph Stalin assured President Roosevelt and British prime minister Winston Churchill that his country would enter the war against Japan three months after the end of the fighting against the Nazis in Europe.

At the time they secured this agreement with Stalin, Roosevelt and U.S. strategists had not known whether the top-secret project to construct an atomic bomb, or A-bomb, would prove successful. In July 1945, U.S. scientists successfully tested an A-bomb in the Nevada desert. On August 6, a U.S. plane dropped an A-bomb on the Japanese city of Hiroshima. Three days later a second bomb was dropped on Nagasaki. The Japanese sued for peace a few days later. But in the meantime, on August 8, three months to the day after the Nazi surrender of May 8, Soviet armies attacked the Japanese in Manchuria.

Soviet Nuclear Weapons
WHY THE KOREAN WAR
DID NOT INVOLVE ATOMIC WARFARE

IN A 1997 BOOK REEVALUATING COLD WAR HISTORY entitled *We Now Know,* John Lewis Gaddis writes: "The taboo on the use of nuclear weapons in limited wars—indeed the very notion of a 'limited' war itself—had not yet taken root [in 1950]; the Korean War defined these principles, but there was little reason to expect, when it broke out, that its conduct would reflect them." U.S. military commanders gave serious consideration to the use of nuclear weapons to stem the Chinese advance, and President Truman publicly threatened their use on one occasion.

One of the things about which it cannot be said "we now know" is the extent to which Soviet possession of the atomic bomb acted as a deterrent to U.S. use of such weapons. The Soviet Union exploded its first nuclear device in the summer of 1949 and had only a few nuclear weapons on hand when the war began. The United States, a nuclear power since 1945, had about 200 bombs in its nuclear arsenal. Nor did the Soviets have any means of delivering a nuclear weapon against the United States, while U.S. long-range bombers were well-positioned to strike Soviet cities. The nuclear balance favored the United States. And yet, had a U.S. nuclear bomb been dropped on Chinese forces in Korea or in Manchuria, the Soviets could have launched a devastating retaliatory strike. Soviet bombers based in Manchuria could have easily hit the Pusan port area, which would have resulted in tens of thousands of U.S. casualties and millions of Korean deaths. One of the things now known is that the Korean War set off a nuclear arms race between the rival superpowers; by war's end the United States had 800 bombs in its arsenal, the Soviet Union, 200.

In their wartime meetings, the leaders of the United States, the Soviet Union, and Great Britain had devoted a great deal of time to discussing postwar borders and the political future of the liberated countries of Europe. They paid relatively little attention to other parts of the world where their armies were fighting. At the Yalta Conference in 1945, Roosevelt proposed that some sort of "trusteeship" be set up to rule over Korea after the war. Stalin agreed, though he said he hoped the period of trusteeship would be a short one. Plans for Korea's future remained vague. U.S. and Soviet military strategists agreed that, once the Red Army entered the war against the Japanese, it would continue its drive into Korea.

By mid-August 1945 U.S. policy makers were having second thoughts. They did not want Korea turned into an outpost of Soviet power after the war. To forestall the possibility that the Russians would simply take over all of Korea, they decided to land U.S. troops at the port of Inchon on Korea's western coast and have them move north to meet the Soviets midway up the peninsula. The two armies would meet along the 38th parallel, which ran about 25 miles north of Inchon and the inland Korean capital of Seoul. In 1945, 9 million Koreans lived north of this line, while 21 million lived south of it. Most of Korea's industry was concentrated north of the line, and most of its agricultural land lay south of it. Until plans could be worked out for an independent, unified Korean government, the Americans and the Soviets would set up occupation governments in the two zones of the country. These plans were similar to those that had been worked out earlier for the postwar occupation of Germany. The difference was that Korea was supposed to be a "liberated" rather than a "defeated" country. Many Koreans resented the fact that the 35-year occupation of their country by one foreign army, the Japanese, was followed immediately by occupation by two new foreign armies.

At first the occupation of Korea went smoothly. Although the Red Army arrived in the country a month before the Americans, the Russians halted their advance, as agreed, at the 38th parallel. U.S. troops under the command of Lt. Gen. John R. Hodge landed at Inchon on September 8, 1945. They marched to Seoul the next day, where they accepted the surrender of the Japanese. The Koreans cheered the arrival of the Americans. But Hodge, a tough and undiplomatic veteran of the fighting on Guadalcanal and Okinawa, angered many Koreans when he decided to leave the Japanese colonial government in power until other arrangements could be made to maintain law and order. After 35 years, even a few more weeks of Japanese rule seemed intolerable. Although Hodge's policy was soon reversed on orders from Washington, it gave a good indication of U.S. priorities in Korea, which emphasized political stability rather than Korean self-determination.

As the cold war intensified in the months after Japan's surrender, the chances for peacefully reuniting the two Korean occupation zones became increasingly unlikely. In the northern half of Korea, Kim Il

Sung's Communists created a government and society along the Soviet model. They divided up the big landholding estates and redistributed land to the peasants, which was a popular move. At the same time they stamped out all opposition to Communist rule, arresting and imprisoning their opponents.

In the southern half of Korea General Hodge, who would remain the U.S. military governor in Korea for four years, was determined to keep the Communists from gaining power. He allied the United States with the most conservative political groups in southern Korea, including those which had collaborated with the Japanese. He ordered the disbanding of the "people's committees," set up after the war by Communists and other independence groups in many Korean cities, as well as communist-influenced labor unions. The Korean national police force arrested and killed thousands of Communists and other opponents of the U.S. military government.

Hodge was on hand to welcome Syngman Rhee back from his long exile in October 1945. U.S. relations with Rhee over the next few years proved stormy, for the cantankerous old man had a mind of his own. "President Syngman Rhee is a man of strong convictions and has little patience with those who differ with him," President Truman recalled in his memoirs. "I did not care for the methods used by Rhee's police to break up political meetings and control political enemies." But in the end Truman decided Rhee was the best available candidate to stiffen the resistance of the anticommunist forces in the South.

American military leaders were not at all enthusiastic about the prospect of tying up tens of thousands of U.S. soldiers on indefinite occupation duty in southern Korea. Preoccupied with the possibility of war breaking out in Europe against Soviet forces, they regarded the Korean Peninsula as a drain on scarce resources, with little strategic significance of its own. The Pentagon pushed for the earliest possible withdrawal from South Korea. The Soviets would pull out their own forces from northern Korea in 1948, leaving behind a large and well equipped North Korean army. However, several thousand Soviet soldiers remained behind as military advisers.

Others in the government were equally determined to maintain a strong U.S. presence in Korea. In September 1946, a half-year before the declaration of the Truman Doctrine, U.S. presidential aide Clark Clifford in a report to the president identified Korea as one of the "trouble spots" where the United States should be prepared to confront the

Kim Il Sung's 1949–1950 Conversations with Stalin

THE OPENING OF SOVIET DIPLOMATIC ARCHIVES IN THE 1990s shed new light on the origins of the Korean War. The initiative for the North Korean attack on South Korea came from North Korean leader Kim Il Sung, who over a period of months in 1949–50 won over a skeptical Joseph Stalin to support the invasion plan. Kim first broached the topic during a meeting with Stalin in Moscow in the spring of 1949. As late as January 1950, Stalin remained unpersuaded, although he did approve stepped-up military assistance to North Korea. "I understand the dissatisfaction of Comrade Kim Il Sung," he cabled the Soviet ambassador in Pyongyang, "but he must understand that such a large matter in regard to South Korea such as he wants to undertake needs large preparation. The matter must be organized so that there would not be too great a risk." The risk that Stalin feared the most was the possibility of a direct military confrontation with the United States.

Stalin did not reveal his intentions to Chinese Communist leader Mao Zedong, whom he met in Moscow in February 1950. Mao would complain several years later to the Soviet ambassador to China that "when I was in Moscow there was no talk about conquering South Korea. . . . But afterwards Kim Il Sung was in Moscow, where a certain agreement was reached about which nobody deemed it necessary to consult with me beforehand."

The "certain agreement" Mao referred to was reached when Kim returned to Moscow in April 1950. While approving the invasion, a still cautious Stalin warned Kim that "if you should get kicked in the teeth," he could not expect to be bailed out militarily by the Soviet Union. Kim would have to turn for help to China instead.

threat of Soviet expansionism. The U.S. State Department argued against any quick withdrawal of U.S. forces from southern Korea, believing that such action would be an invitation for a Communist takeover or invasion.

In May 1948 the United Nations, at the request of the United States and over the objections of the Soviet Union, organized parliamentary elections in South Korea. North Korea refused to participate, and communists in South Korea called for a boycott of the elections. The new

Syngman Rhee (1875–1965), newly elected chairman of the Republic of Korea's National Assembly, delivers the opening address at its first meeting on May 31, 1948. *(U.S. Army Military History Institute)*

South Korean National Assembly elected Syngman Rhee as its chairman and in July adopted a constitution establishing the Republic of Korea in the South. General MacArthur made a rare trip away from his headquarters in Japan to attend Rhee's inauguration in Seoul. Rhee clamped down on critics of his regime, arresting almost 90,000 people between the fall of 1948 and the spring of 1949. North Korea's Communists responded to the events in the South by setting up their own government, the Democratic People's Republic of Korea (DPRK), in July 1948. U.S. occupation of Korea formally ended in August 1948. Apart from a few hundred U.S. military advisers (known as the Korean Military Advisory Group, or KMAG), all U.S. troops had been withdrawn from South Korea by the end of June 1949.

Neither the South Koreans under Syngman Rhee nor the North Koreans under Kim Il Sung recognized the legitimacy of the other's government. Fighting frequently broke out on the border between the two countries, with small groups launching raids against each other's lines. Rhee made his U.S. allies nervous by repeatedly announcing his intention to march on the North and unify all of Korea under his own leadership. As a result, the United States restricted the kinds of aid it provided the new ROK army. The South Koreans were given small arms, light artillery, and tons of ammunition but no tanks or aircraft. The United States wanted to see the ROK forces strong enough to repel a North Korean attack but too weak to launch an offensive of their own. Kim Il Sung faced no such restrictions in building up his own military forces. By the spring of 1950 North Korea had 135,000 soldiers, many of them battle-hardened veterans of the fighting in Manchuria during the Chinese Revolution and they were equipped with Soviet T-34 tanks and heavy artillery. The South Koreans had fewer than half as many soldiers.

In the five years that followed the World War II, Korea was a country at war with itself. In those years, as many as 100,000 Koreans died in the fighting between Kim Il Sung and Syngman Rhee's sympathizers. This bloody "peace" came to an end shortly before dawn on Sunday, June 25, 1950, when ROK lines along the 38th parallel came under a heavy artillery barrage. Within hours North Korean tanks and infantry had broken through South Korean lines and were on their way to Seoul. The Korean War had begun. Task Force Smith would soon be on its way to the front.

3

DEFEAT AND RETREAT

It was against this background, drawing on these historical roots, that the North Korean People's Army (NKPA) unleashed a devastating artillery barrage across the 38th parallel in those predawn hours of June 25, 1950. Within days, Task Force Smith would be thrown into the front lines. But long before they could be on the scene, immediately after the artillery barrage lifted, some 90,000 NKPA soldiers, supported by more than 100 fighter planes and 150 tanks, poured across the border into South Korea. As Republic of Korea (ROK) defenses broke in the onslaught of the first few hours, North Korean leader Kim Il Sung spoke to his people on the radio. He claimed it was South Korea that had invaded the North, and that NKPA soldiers were merely responding to the aggression of the "bandit traitor Syngman Rhee."

As soon as he learned of the attack, the U.S. ambassador to South Korea sent a coded cable to Washington. "According to Korean army reports," the cable said, "North Korean forces invaded the Republic of Korea territory at several points this morning . . . It would appear from the nature of the attack and the manner in which it was launched that it constitutes an all-out offensive against the Republic of Korea." It was late at night on the evening of June 24, Washington, D.C., time, when the cable arrived and was decoded in the State Department.

No one in the State Department or the Pentagon had been expecting trouble to break out so soon in Korea. U.S. intelligence reports in the weeks preceding June 25 failed to note any special military preparations by North Korea. U.S. president Harry Truman was not even in

Washington to receive the news. He was relaxing at his family home in Independence, Missouri, when he was called that night by Secretary of State Dean Acheson. Acheson suggested to the president that the United States call for a special meeting of the UN Security Council to discuss the attack. It was the United Nations, after all, that had created the Republic of Korea just two years earlier. Truman and Acheson's decision to turn to the United Nations would have great significance in shaping the coming war.

In Tokyo General MacArthur learned of the attack soon after it began. He told John Foster Dulles, a prominent Republican leader who was there on a special diplomatic mission for the president, that "If Washington only will not hobble me, I can handle [the invasion] with one arm tied behind my back." Dulles cabled Acheson, urging U.S. intervention. Syngman Rhee sent his own message to Truman asking for aid.

There had never been a U.S. commitment to go to war to defend South Korea. In fact, in a speech to the National Press Club in Washington the previous January, Secretary of State Acheson had described the "defense line" the United States was committed to defending in the Pacific in such a way that it seemed to exclude South Korea altogether. Republicans later charged that Acheson's speech in January had encouraged Kim Il Sung's decision to invade in June, conveniently ignoring the fact that in January many Republican congressmen had cast their votes to help defeat a Korean aid bill proposed by the Truman administration. The Pentagon's contingency plans in the event of a North Korean invasion called for the withdrawal of U.S. military and diplomatic personnel from South Korea, rather than fighting it out with invading communists.

Bad news from Korea continued to pour into Washington all day Sunday, June 25 (June 26 in Korea). While Truman prepared to leave Independence, Missouri, Sunday afternoon, the UN Security Council met in Lake Success, New York, to debate the U.S. resolution on the North Korean invasion. (The United Nations had not yet moved into its present, permanent headquarters in New York City.) The UN Security Council was made up of delegates from five permanent member countries (Britain, France, China, the United States, the Soviet Union) and delegates from six other nations. Any one of the permanent members of the Security Council had the right to veto a resolution that came before the council. The Soviet delegate, who ordinarily could have been expected to veto the U.S. resolution condemning North Korea, was absent that Sunday. The Soviets had been boycotting meetings of the UN Security Council since January 1950 to protest the exclusion of Communist China from UN membership. As a result, the UN Security Council voted 9-0, with Yugoslavia abstaining, to call for the immediate withdrawal of North Korean forces from South Korea.

The Soviet absence from the Security Council should have raised doubts in Washington's mind about Moscow's intentions. If this was a carefully planned blow—and perhaps the start of a much larger war—then why had not Soviet leader Joseph Stalin ordered his diplomats to attend the Security Council meetings? (The Soviet delegate would finally return to the Security Council on August 1, too late to undo the earlier UN resolutions on Korea.) The fumbling Soviet diplomatic response to the invasion suggests how little thought Stalin had given to the war and its consequences.

On his flight back to Washington on June 25, Truman recalled in his memoirs, he thought long and hard about how the United States should respond to the North Korean aggression. He was reminded of the events leading up to World War II:

> In my generation, this was not the first occasion when the strong had attacked the weak. I recalled some earlier instances: Manchuria, Ethiopia, Austria. I remembered how each time that the democracies failed to act, it had encouraged the aggressors to keep going ahead. Communism was acting in Korea just as Hitler, Mussolini and the Japanese had acted . . . If this were allowed to go unchallenged it would mean a third World War, just as similar incidents had brought on the Second World War.

But it was not just the memories of World War II that shaped Truman's response. American policy makers were already inclined to intervene to stop the spread of communism before the news arrived from Korea, as the National Security Council's secret report NSC-68 indicates. And Truman had not forgotten the attacks on his administration by Republicans for having "lost" China the previous year to the Communists. He had no intention of seeing his presidency utterly wrecked by now losing Korea as well.

For all these reasons, Truman felt that the moment had come for decisive action. He made a series of decisions over the next few days

Member of Korean Military Advisory Group (KMAG) and his interpreter (right) instruct a Republic of Korea (ROK) Army 60 mm mortar crew. *(U.S. Army Military History Institute)*

committing the United States to confronting the Communists in Korea, and throughout Asia if necessary. At a meeting with his national security advisers on Sunday evening, June 25, Truman authorized the use of U.S. air and naval units to attack North Koreans south of the 38th parallel. On Monday, June 26, he ordered the U.S. Seventh Fleet into the Formosa Strait, the waters that separated the Communist Chinese mainland from the Nationalist Chinese island of Formosa. Truman also decided to increase U.S. military aid to the French forces fighting in Indochina. On Tuesday, June 27, he ordered the U.S. ambassador to the United Nations to propose a new resolution to the Security Council calling for member nations to provide aid to South Korea to resist North Korea's aggression. The Security Council voted late Tuesday evening, with the Soviet Union still absent, to "furnish such assistance . . . as may be necessary to repel the armed attack and to restore international peace and security in the area."

That same day, Truman briefed congressional leaders on the situation in South Korea and his own decisions since the start of the invasion. Although committing the United States to military action, Truman carefully avoided saying that the United States was going to war in Korea. Truman's decision to go to war solely on his own authority as commander in chief of U.S. forces came under harsh criticism from Republican critics in Congress, who accused him of ignoring Congress's constitutional right to declare war. Truman hoped to sidestep the issue by calling U.S. involvement a "police action" rather than a war. This was the United States's first major undeclared foreign war. It was also the first war it fought under a flag other than its own—the blue banner of the United Nations.

On July 7, the UN Security Council voted to establish a United Nations command to coordinate military efforts in defense of South Korea. In recognition of the fact that the United States was doing most of the fighting in the war, Truman was authorized to appoint the commander of UN forces. Truman appointed MacArthur to the post on July 8. Six days later Syngman Rhee placed ROK forces under MacArthur's command. For the moment, apart from some air support from the Australians, the U.S. and ROK soldiers fought alone, but within months soldiers from 15 nations, including Britain and the British Commonwealth, France, Turkey, Greece, and Thailand had joined the Americans in Korea. Several nations, including Britain and Australia, sent naval units to support the efforts of the U.S. fleet off Korea's shores.

In South Korea the situation had been growing more desperate by the hour. The NKPA reached the outskirts of Seoul on Tuesday, June 27. Syngman Rhee and the South Korean government, along with U.S. embassy personnel and military advisers, headed south to avoid capture. The ROK troops fighting a rearguard action in the city were poorly led and disorganized. Thousands of them were cut off from retreat on the early morning of June 28, when a panicky ROK officer prematurely blew up the bridge spanning the Han River south of the city. Hundreds of civilians and soldiers who were crossing the bridge when it was blown were killed in the explosion.

On June 29, Truman, on the urging of the U.S. Joint Chiefs of Staff (JCS), authorized U.S. air and naval strikes north of the 38th parallel. The same day MacArthur made his inspection trip to South Korea and cabled the request to Washington that led to the decision to dispatch Task Force Smith. The first U.S. soldiers ever to confront an Asian com-

DEFEAT AND RETREAT

The battleship USS *Missouri* fires a 16-inch salvo at the enemy to cut lines of communication along North Korea's east coast. *(U.S. Army Military History Institute)*

munist army on the ground were on their way to the front on July 1, in what General MacArthur hoped would prove to be an "arrogant display of strength."

While MacArthur, as supreme commander of UN forces, made his decisions from his headquarters in Tokyo, he dispatched subordinate officers to take command on the ground in Korea. Beginning with his arrival on July 12, the senior U.S. commander in Korea was Lt. Gen. Walton A. Walker, a highly regarded combat veteran of both World War I and II who had served as commander of the U.S. Eighth Army in Japan since 1948. Walker took command in Korea on his arrival on July 12. As Walker's troops arrived in Korea, they became known as the Eighth U.S. Army, Korea, or EUSAK.

The first U.S. unit to fight in Korea was the army's Twenty-fourth Infantry Division, including the men of Task Force Smith and the Twenty-first and Thirty-fourth Infantry Regiments. In three weeks of heavy fighting in July, the Twenty-fourth would be battered and decimated by the North Koreans. The only thing the Americans could do in

KOREAN WAR

The Twenty-fourth Infantry Regiment moves into battle in Korea, July 18, 1950. *(National Archives/DOD, War and Conflict, #1385)*

the short run in Korea was to trade space for time, delaying the enemy's advance down the peninsula as long as possible while more troops and equipment unloaded from ships and planes in the southern port city of Pusan. The Twenty-fourth Division was under the command of Maj. Gen. William F. Dean, a hefty six-footer and decorated combat veteran of World War II. Dean had served as U.S. military governor in South Korea for a year in the late 1940s, before assuming command of the Twenty-fourth Infantry Division in Japan in 1949. While Task Force Smith was being swept aside, Dean's forces took up positions farther south, along the road from Seoul.

The men of the Thirty-fourth Infantry Regiment were the next to learn just what a formidable enemy the North Koreans could be. They were not ready for battle. Their artillery support was still being unloaded from ships in Pusan when they took their positions two miles north of Pyongtaek and about 10 miles south of Task Force Smith's position. Some of the men of the Thirty-fourth had not yet fired the M-1 rifles they had been issued; only when they saw the North Koreans advancing did they discover that the rifles were defective.

DEFEAT AND RETREAT

On July 6 the Americans fought a brief skirmish along a stream north of Pyongtaek. Col. Jay B. Lovless, who had commanded the Thirty-fourth Infantry for only a month before the start of the war, ordered his men to withdraw to secure positions about 15 miles farther south rather than risk the fate of Task Force Smith. (His orders were unclear as to whether and how long he was to hold his position in the face of a determined enemy attack.) The retreat turned into a disorderly rout, with soldiers discarding their weapons, helmets, and even their shoes along the way. Marguerite Higgins (the only female war correspondent in Korea) reported seeing "young Americans turn and bolt in battle, or throw down their arms cursing their government for what they thought was embroilment in a hopeless cause . . ." An enraged General Dean sacked Lovless as commander of the Thirty-fourth on July 7. Lovless's replacement, Col. Robert Martin, had arrived in Korea only the day before. He was killed in action July 8, cut in half by tank fire while trying to destroy a North Korean tank with a bazooka. The Thirty-fourth Infantry Regiment once again pulled back in panic.

Infantryman in foreground loads new clip into his M-1 rifle, as his companion fires at the enemy. *(Lyndon Baines Johnson Library & Museum)*

Marguerite Higgins,
war correspondent
(Library of Congress)

North Koreans were now advancing virtually unopposed down Korea's west coast. The farther south they got, the more side roads opened up from the main road leading from Seoul, and this increased the opportunity for outflanking the Americans. Every time the Americans set up a defensive line, they found themselves brushed aside with heavy casualties. The North Koreans succeeded with a simple tactic. They would hit the Americans head-on with tanks, then outflank them with infantry, getting behind U.S. positions to cut off their retreat. The Americans also found it hard to cope with the thousands of civilian refugees who clogged the roads. Sometimes North Korean soldiers wearing civilian clothes mixed in with the refugees, infiltrating U.S. lines and attacking from the rear. Jittery U.S. soldiers began firing on oncoming civilians, with many innocent lives lost. General Dean soon developed a respect for the fighting qualities of the North Koreans; he compared stopping their advance to "trying to keep water from coming through a fishnet." General MacArthur, dismayed by the steady retreat of his forces down the peninsula, cabled the Joint Chiefs of Staff urging that at least four more divisions of U.S. troops be sent to Korea as soon as possible.

North Koreans crossed the Kum River on July 14 and 15, another disaster for the Americans. U.S. commanders had hoped to hold the North Koreans at the river, which flowed 10 miles east of the strategically important city of Taejon and served as a kind of defensive moat. All the bridges along the river had been blown up by U.S. engineers, but the North Koreans crossed the river in barges on July 14, overrunning the Sixty-third Field Artillery Battalion, capturing 10 105 mm howitzers and killing or capturing more than 100 men. On July 16, the North Koreans hit the Nineteenth Infantry Regiment, just sent to reinforce the line, a regiment known as "The Rock of Chickamauga" for its famous stand in a bloody Civil War battle. Hit from the front and along their exposed flank, the "Chicks" were forced back in disorder. Half of the regiment's 900 men were killed or missing at the end of the day's battle. One rifle company suffered 122 casualties out of 171 men who went into the battle.

Refugee columns moving south often served as cover for North Korean infiltrators. *(Lyndon Baines Johnson Library & Museum)*

General Dean made his personal final stand against the North Koreans in the battle for control of the crucial crossroads city of Tae-jon, 100 miles south of Seoul, on July 19–20. Dean had set up his command center in Taejon, the sixth largest city in South Korea, when he arrived in the country on July 3. As the North Koreans crossed the Kum, Dean decided to pull out the 4,000 U.S. defenders of the city, but on July 18 General Walker asked him to hold Taejon for two more days to allow the newly arrived U.S. First Cavalry Division time to deploy its forces. Dean's Twenty-fourth Division had recently been issued some of the army's new 3.5-inch rocket launchers, which he hoped would

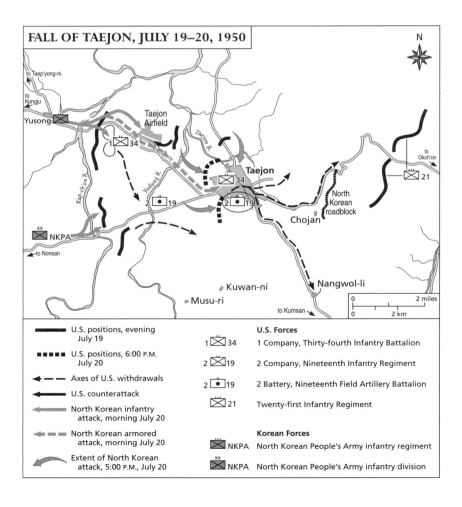

FALL OF TAEJON, JULY 19–20, 1950

N

to Taep'yong-ni

to Kongju

Yusong

Taejon Airfield

1 ⊠ 34

Taejon R.

Kap-ch'on R.

Yudung R.

Taejon

34

to Okch'on

⊠ 21

North Korean roadblock

2 ⊠ 19

2 ⊡ 19

Chojan

××
⊠ NKPA

to Nonsan

Kuwan-ni

Musu-ri

Nangwol-li

to Kumsan

0   2 miles
0   2 km

U.S. positions, evening July 19

U.S. positions, 6:00 P.M. July 20

Axes of U.S. withdrawals

U.S. counterattack

North Korean infantry attack, morning July 20

North Korean armored attack, morning July 20

Extent of North Korean attack, 5:00 P.M., July 20

U.S. Forces

1 ⊠ 34   1 Company, Thirty-fourth Infantry Battalion

2 ⊠ 19   2 Company, Nineteenth Infantry Regiment

2 ⊡ 19   2 Battery, Nineteenth Field Artillery Battalion

⊠ 21   Twenty-first Infantry Regiment

Korean Forces

⊠ NKPA   North Korean People's Army infantry regiment

⊠ NKPA   North Korean People's Army infantry division

DEFEAT AND RETREAT

Combat medics work to save the life of a wounded soldier.
(National Archives)

give his troops, for the first time, the ability to stop the North Koreans'
T-34 tanks.

The battle for the city started July 19. North Koreans again attacked
from the front while encircling the city from the south. North Korea's
YAK fighter planes bombed and strafed the city and dropped propaganda leaflets calling on the Americans to surrender. North Korean
heavy artillery pounded the city. By the early morning of July 20, three
columns of North Korean tanks and infantry had broken into the city.
A hard and bloody and confusing street battle followed in the burning
city. Dean, exhausted, had no real idea of how the battle was going.
Instead, he went out into the streets and fought bravely if not wisely as
an infantryman. "Very few of the things I did [during the battle of Tae-
jon] could not have been done by any competent sergeant," he later
wrote. Dean went "tank hunting" with a bazooka team, and at one point
was seen firing his .45 automatic pistol at a tank. Small groups of Amer-

icans managed to break out of the city during the day, on foot or in jeeps and trucks.

At dusk, having ordered the city evacuated, Dean made what seemed like a miraculous escape through heavy enemy fire, careening through the streets and around burning trucks and tanks in his jeep. Later he had to abandon his jeep and take to the hills. Cut off from U.S. lines, Dean was captured by the North Koreans after five weeks of wandering through the hills, during which time he almost starved to death. Dean was the highest-ranking U.S. prisoner of war (POW) held by the North Koreans. Awarded the Medal of Honor for his part in the defense of Taejon, Dean later wrote that "I wouldn't have awarded myself a wooden star for what I did as a commander." At the end of the battle of Taejon, more than 1,100 Americans were left killed, wounded, or missing.

In three weeks of fighting, during which the Twenty-fourth Division was forced to retreat 100 miles, the Americans suffered heavily. Many lives were thrown away due to overconfidence and military blunders. But the young and inexperienced soldiers did buy time for reinforcements to arrive. During the Twenty-fourth's bitter retreat, the Twenty-fifth Infantry Division and the First Cavalry Division landed in Korea. There were still too few Americans and too many North Koreans. After the battle of Taejon the remnants of the Twenty-fourth Division were

A wounded marine is placed in a carrier attached to a Sikorsky H-5 helicopter for transport to a field hospital.
(National Archives)

relieved by the First Cavalry. But after only a day in reserve, the exhausted men had to be thrown back into battle to block a threatened enemy envelopment of the Eighth Army's western flank.

U.S. soldiers suffered from the heat, from illness caused by drinking dirty water from the rice paddies, from insects, from a lack of food and dry clothing, and from poor physical conditioning. Pfc. Leonard Korgie of the Thirty-fourth Infantry remembered the intense heat and thirst and the lack of rest: "You can't think when you're as fatigued as we were. I just sensed we were going to find another hill and be attacked, then find another hill and so forth, endlessly, forever. Where was it going to end? Weren't there any other GIs in this Army?"

The new troops rushed to the front suffered repeated defeats. The First Cavalry Division (which had been reorganized as an infantry division in World War II) landed in Korea on July 18 and went into battle soon after. It was bloodied in its first battle at Yongdong on July 24–25 and disappointed U.S. commanders, who had expected great things from the celebrated unit. Another unlucky unit was the Twenty-fourth Infantry Regiment of the Twenty-fifth Division, which landed in Korea on July 13. This was an all-black unit. (Despite President Truman's order to desegregate the armed forces in 1948, the army still maintained segregated units at the start of the Korean War.) Elements of the Twenty-fourth had performed bravely in a battle at Yechon on July 20, the U.S. Army's first successful counterattack in the war. But on July 22, near Sangju, another unit of the Twenty-fourth Regiment withdrew from the battlefield after a sharp fight with the NKPA that cost the Americans 27 dead and nearly 300 wounded. The controversy over whether or not the unit "panicked" at Sangju remains hotly debated among historians and veterans of the action, but there is no question that the Twenty-fourth's withdrawal caused many white soldiers in Korea to question whether black soldiers would stand and fight. However, given the generally uneven to poor performance of U.S. units in the early days of the war, it is unfair to single out the black soldiers of the Twenty-fourth for criticism.

The worst setback after the battle of Taejon was the destruction of the Third Battalion of the Twenty-ninth Infantry Regiment. This was a unit that had been doing garrison duty on Okinawa, and it was filled with green and poorly trained troops. Arriving in Korea July 24, they were ordered to advance on the town of Hadong two days later. Their truck convoy was ambushed by the North Koreans July 27. Of the

End of Segregation in the U.S. Military

THE UNITED STATES FOUGHT WORLD WAR II WITH A segregated army that relegated its African-American citizen soldiers, sailors, and airmen to second-class status. Blacks served in segregated units, usually commanded by white officers. Demands for equal treatment met little sympathy from senior military commanders, who argued that the armed forces was no place to try out "risky" social experiments.

But the hypocrisy of asking blacks to defend freedom while denying them equal opportunity in military service sparked demands for change. In 1947 the labor leader and civil rights activist A. Philip Randolph organized the Committee Against Jim Crow in Military Service and Training, calling on African Americans to refuse to register for the draft as long as the U.S. armed forces remained segregated. Its slogan was "Don't Join a Jim Crow Army!" In 1948 President Harry S. Truman issued an executive order directing the armed forces to desegregate. The military, especially the army, was slow to comply, and when the Korean War broke out, the United States once again fielded a segregated military force.

Custom and prejudice finally gave way before the demands for manpower. By early 1951 black soldiers began to be assigned as replacements to white units fighting in Korea; more and more the units of fresh troops sent to the conflict consisted of whites and blacks who had trained together in the United States. Late in 1951 the all-black Twenty-fourth Infantry Regiment, which had been one of the first army units sent to Korea, was disbanded and its soldiers sent to serve alongside

unit's 757 men, more than 300 were killed and 100 more captured in the attack. The Twenty-ninth Infantry's First Battalion was cut off by the North Koreans that same day in another action, suffering an additional 215 casualties.

One of the few U.S. units to perform well its first time in combat was the Twenty-fifth Division's Twenty-seventh ("Wolfhound") Infantry Regiment, under the command of Lt. Col. John "Iron Mike" Michaelis, who as a young officer in World War II had parachuted into Normandy with the

white soldiers in other outfits. At the end of October 1954, 15 months after the end of the Korean War, the U.S. Army was at last able to report that it contained no more racially segregated units.

Gen. Douglas MacArthur inspecting troops of the Twenty-fourth Infantry on his arrival at Kimpo airfield for a tour of the battlefront *(National Archives)*

101st Airborne Division. Michaelis's Wolfhounds skillfully fended off a North Korean attack near Hwanggan on July 24–25, destroying six T-34 tanks and killing many North Korean infantrymen before their orderly withdrawal in the face of overwhelming enemy forces.

Having had everything their way since the start of the war, the North Koreans apparently grew overconfident. With the Eighth Army on the run, the North Korean commanders decided to divide their forces. Two of the best North Korean divisions were sent south to the

The No Gun Ri Controversy

IN 1999 THE ASSOCIATED PRESS REPORTED THAT, IN THE early days of the Korean War, U.S. soldiers and warplanes had massacred some 400 South Korean refugees near the village of No Gun Ri, south of Seoul. According to reports by Korean civilians, buttressed by the testimony of an American veteran named Edward Lee Daily, a column of civilians was bombed and strafed by U.S. planes on July 26, 1950. The survivors were then herded by soldiers from the U.S. Army's First Cavalry Division into two nearby railroad tunnels, where they were fired upon by U.S. soldiers over the next four days, resulting in an additional 300 deaths. According to Daily, the shooting of civilians was on direct orders of U.S. officers.

The report stirred controversy. In the months that followed, the U.S. Army undertook its own review of the events at No Gun Ri, interviewing hundreds of U.S. veterans. The army's review team concluded that an undetermined number of South Korean refugees had, indeed, been killed by U.S. personnel in the vicinity of No Gun Ri, but that the numbers involved had probably been exaggerated. The army denied that any orders had ever been issued targeting civilians. Instead, it attributed the killings to the panic and inexperience of U.S. soldiers caught up in the retreat before the North Korean onslaught. According to the official report, "given the fact that many of the U.S. soldiers lacked combat-experienced officers and non-commissioned officers, some soldiers may have fired out of fear in response to a perceived enemy threat without considering the possibility that they might be firing on Korean civilians." It also turned out that Edward Lee Daily had lied about his combat experience and presence at No Gun Ri, casting further doubt on the original report.

Korean coast, to attempt an envelopment of Pusan. This was a major blunder, for it slowed the main North Korean advance and gave the Americans time to prepare new defenses.

On July 29, General Walker issued a "stand or die" order to his troops. He declared that "There is no line behind us to which we can retreat . . . [A] retreat to Pusan would be one of the greatest butcheries in history. We must fight until the end." In fact, U.S. units continued to pull back for the next few days to the Naktong River, a natural defensive line. The delay in the North Korean advance for the first time in the war gave U.S. soldiers time to prepare. They now had adequate supplies, air support, and clear interior lines of communication. U.S. troops could be moved swiftly and easily within the remaining corner of Korea they controlled. General Walker shifted men of the Twenty-fifth Division from the northern front at Taegu, where NKPA pressure had lessened, to the threatened southwestern front. Army engineers blew up the last bridge crossing the Naktong on August 2, a month and a day after the men of Task Force Smith stepped off their planes in Korea. The Americans had suffered more than 6,000 casualties since the start of the war, including nearly 1,900 dead; 900 Americans had been taken as prisoners of war. ROK forces were even harder hit, having suffered 70,000 casualties.

U.S. troops now defended what became known as the "Pusan Perimeter." This was an area of southeastern Korea about 50 miles wide and 100 miles deep, backing on to the sea on the east and south, with the Naktong River along its western edge, and a rugged mountain chain along its northern flank. The ROK held the north, while the Eighth Army held the western flank. The North Koreans had enjoyed the ini-

Ninety mm antiaircraft guns are fired as field artillery in support of ROK forces north of Taegu. *(U.S. Army Military History Institute)*

tiative since June 25, but they were no longer the fighting force they had been on that day. The NKPA had suffered almost 60,000 casualties since the start of the war and had lost two-thirds of its heavy T-34 tanks. Within a few days after the Pusan Perimeter was established, the UN defenders actually outnumbered the NKPA attackers. The tide of battle was about to turn.

4

PUSAN AND
INCHON

———◆—∞————————————————————

The late summer and early autumn of 1950 brought a dramatic reversal in the fortunes of war in Korea. The triumphant North Korean advance ground to a halt in August at the edge of the Pusan Perimeter. The Eighth Army and its South Korean allies, after weeks of retreat, turned and fought the enemy to a standstill in six weeks of bloody defensive battles. And in mid-September General MacArthur launched a bold invasion of the port of Inchon, putting the United Nations on the offensive for the first time in the war. Within two weeks of the landings at Inchon, Seoul had been liberated and the North Korean army had been swept out of South Korea. Had the fighting ended on September 30, 1950, the Korean War would be remembered today as one of the greatest triumphs of U.S. arms.

At the start of August, the prospects for such a smashing UN victory could not have looked more remote. By August 2 all of South Korea, except for the 5,000-square-mile rectangle of land known as the Pusan Perimeter, had fallen to the Communists. If the NKPA could cross the Naktong River in force, or sweep down from the northern mountains, they could drive the Americans and their allies into the sea. As Eighth Army commander Walton Walker reminded his men, there was no further room for retreat.

Walker threw every available man into the fighting. The battered veterans of July's battles were reinforced as quickly as ships and planes could carry U.S. and allied forces across the Pacific. More than 200 ships unloaded their cargoes of men and supplies in Pusan in the last two

Fresh and eager U.S. Marine troops, newly arrived at the vital southern supply port of Pusan, are shown prior to moving up to the front lines, August 1950. *(National Archives/DOD, War and Conflict, #1386)*

weeks of July. The U.S. Army's Second Infantry Division, the First Provisional Marine Brigade, and the British Twenty-seventh Brigade all arrived in August. When the soldiers climbed off the boats in Pusan, they were often sent directly to the front lines. Green and untried troops quickly absorbed the lessons of their first battles, or else they died. The horrors of war grew familiar. Marine private Doug Koch spent a hot day in August carrying the bodies of dead buddies back to his unit's command post:

> I'd never handled a body before nor had the other two Marines with me . . . I learned that day about the smell of death. A dead person smells different than a dead animal and the smell is something you never forget. It's something that can't be put on television or in the newsreels. They can capture the sound and some of the confusion of battle, but the smell of death is something they can't record.

The North Koreans remained on the offensive but knew that they were racing against time. Every passing day brought more U.S. soldiers, tanks, guns, and aircraft into the fight. The Communists had to win quickly if they were going to win at all. And to do so they were willing to pay virtually any price in the lives of their own soldiers. They probed constantly for weak spots in the defense of the Pusan Perimeter, and when they found one they hit it with "human wave assaults." In these attacks, wave after wave of North Korean attackers would continue charging and dying until the U.S. defenders ran out of ammunition and were overwhelmed.

Walker did not have enough troops to maintain a continuous defensive line around the Pusan Perimeter. But he was able to keep some troops in reserve behind the front lines, shifting them around as needed, anticipating or responding to enemy attacks. One of the most serious North Korean challenges came at a place called the Naktong Bulge, a stretch of the river where it looped westward. Infantry from the crack North Korean Fourth Division, which had brushed past Task Force Smith early in the war, waded across the shoulder-deep water of the Naktong early on the morning of August 6. They moved trucks and tanks and heavy artillery across the river on rafts and by means of an underwater bridge they constructed. From their beachhead on the east side of the river thousands of North Koreans climbed up onto the series of high ridges that led eastward toward Pusan. First Lt. Charles Payne of the Thirty-fourth Infantry had encountered the NKPA's

Fourth Division before, in the fighting up near Osan in early July. Now he was once again fighting for his life, firing at the North Koreans from inside the flimsy shelter of a tin-sided gristmill:

> Hour after hour we held the North Koreans off. At first we let them get within eight or ten feet of the mill. Then we'd fire a volley and the enemy would fall back. Heavy fighting for hours. We used all our grenades. Time and time again the gooks rushed us. Each time we'd lose a man, the gooks would lose many. In front of the mill, the ground was covered with their dead. We stacked our dead around us for protection. The battle seemed to go on forever.

Badly wounded, Payne survived the attack and was awarded a Silver Star for his heroism. The North Korean attack stalled in the face of such fierce resistance, but as long as they held onto their beachhead and the hills beyond, they represented a dagger pointed at the port of Pusan, only about 30 miles to the east.

U.S. army units launched several unsuccessful counterattacks. On August 17, the First Provisional Marine Brigade was given the

Mobilization of
U.S. Reserves in Korea

COL. HARRY G. SUMMERS, A KOREAN WAR VETERAN and military historian, argues that "Without mobilization of its reserve military forces, the United States would have lost the Korean War." The U.S. Army and Marine Corps units available to be rushed to Korea in the summer of 1950 were often woefully under strength; although draft calls were dramatically increased that summer, it would take many months to call up and train draftees. Instead, the U.S. military relied heavily on its reserve forces, the overwhelming majority of whom were veterans of the World War II. These were men who could be sent into battle without extensive preparation. Many of those who served were rushed to Korea as reinforcements and replacements for regular military units already committed to battle. Nearly one in five of the marines who landed at Inchon in September 1950, for example, were men called up from the reserves.

Rocket man of Second Battalion, Seventh Marines, launches a difficult shot against North Koreans dug in on hillside. *(National Archives)*

assignment of spearheading the attack in the Naktong Bulge. The marines had to drive the North Koreans out of the series of high ridges overlooking the Naktong River. The toughest battle was fought for control of a mile-and-a-half-long ridge called Obong-ni, which the Marines referred to as "No Name Ridge" or, more graphically, "Bloody Ridge." After marine Corsair fighters plastered the North Korean defenders, the marines headed up the side of the hill. Marine commander Gen. Edward Craig watched through binoculars as his troops fought their way forward, while the North Koreans poured machine-gun fire and grenades down on them. "I never saw men with so much guts," he said at one point in that long day. The North Koreans sent in four T-34 tanks against the marines on Obong-ni, but U.S. bazookas, Pershing tanks, and fighter planes knocked them all out. By the end of the day the marines had gained the high ground, and they withstood heavy North Korean counterattacks that left hundreds of Korean bodies piled up in front of their positions. The next day the marines moved down the ridge and cleared off the remaining enemy force. Sixty-six marines were killed and nearly 300 were wounded in the attack on Obong-ni. The North Koreans' Fourth Division was virtually destroyed in the battle.

In the northwest sector of the Pusan Perimeter, the Communists launched repeated assaults against the city of Taegu, an important rail center and site of Eighth Army headquarters. Fortunately for the defenders of the Pusan Perimeter, the Communists made the mistake of dividing their own forces in an attempt to keep up pressure on several fronts at once. General Walker was able to move his reserve units, or "fire brigades" as they were called, into areas where the Communists threatened to break through. Soldiers from the First Cavalry Division turned back North Korean assaults across the Naktong on August 9, August 12, and August 14. The ROKs lost control of the town of Pohang-dong on August 10, but Americans rushed to the area and retook the town 10 days later.

Some of the hardest fighting in this sector took place along the Taegu-Sanjy road. A mile-long stretch of the road ran through a river valley flanked by steep hills and was known to U.S. soldiers as the "Bowling Alley." Beginning August 18, and for the next six nights, North Korean infantry and T-34 tanks tried to push their way down the Bowling Alley toward Taegu. The "Wolfhounds" of Col. "Iron Mike"

Cleaning out enemy entrenchments, such as the hillside bunker shown here, made battles long and bloody. *(Lyndon Baines Johnson Library & Museum)*

Ninth Infantry soldiers ride an M-26 Pershing tank into battle on the
Naktong Perimeter, September 1950. *(U.S. Army Military History Institute)*

Michaelis's Twenty-seventh Infantry Regiment held the high ground
above the road. They fought the North Koreans to a standstill night
after night, with artillery and Pershing tanks taking a heavy toll on
the attackers.

In a last desperate push on August 31, the North Koreans launched
coordinated attacks on the U.S. Twenty-fifth Division, Second Division,
and First Cavalry. Once again NKPA soldiers poured across the Naktong
River into the Bulge, retaking the ridges that the marines had spent so
many lives clearing out two weeks earlier. Pohang-dong fell again, Taegu
was threatened, and the safety of the entire Pusan Perimeter seemed in
doubt. But North Korean resources in men, ammunition, and supplies
were stretched to the limit. They could not exploit their temporary
gains on the ground. The marines once again fought their way up
Bloody Ridge in the Naktong Bulge, while the army rolled back the
assault on other fronts. The NKPA's last offensive of the war petered out
by the second week in September.

In the meantime, preparations for a U.S. attack known as Operation
Chromite were reaching their final stages. The target of the operation
was the port city of Inchon. Inchon was located on the Yellow Sea at the
mouth of the Han River, 180 miles northwest of the Pusan Perimeter
and some 25 miles west of Seoul. By means of an amphibious landing
at Inchon, far behind enemy lines, General MacArthur was convinced

Canada's Role in the Korean War

CANADA SUPPLIED MORE THAN 20,000 SOLDIERS TO the UN Command in the Korean War, as well as naval and air force units. All of the Canadians who were sent to fight in Korea were volunteers. The first Canadians to see action were sailors on the destroyer *Cayuga*, which bombarded North Korean soldiers driving southward toward Pusan in August 1950. A number of other Canadian destroyers took part in the blockade of the Korean coastline; in September 1952 the destroyer *Nootka* captured a North Korean mine-laying vessel—the only time in the war when a North Korean ship would be taken at sea.

In December 1950 the Second Battalion, Princess Patricia's Canadian Light Infantry, was the first unit of Canadian ground forces to arrive in Korea. The Canadian soldiers moved to the front in February 1951 and saw heavy fighting in April when they helped beat back the Chinese spring offensive. Later arrivals were organized into the Canadian Twenty-fifth Infantry Brigade, which served as part of the highly regarded First British Commonwealth Division.

The Royal Canadian Air Force (RCAF) supplied a transport squadron to the UN Command, which flew supply runs. In addition, 22 RCAF fighter pilots were assigned to U.S. squadrons; altogether the Canadian pilots were credited with 20 kills of enemy aircraft.

Although their soldiers fought side by side, the Canadian and U.S. governments did not always see eye to eye on the strategy and conduct of the war. Canada opposed any plans to extend the war beyond the boundaries of the Korean Peninsula, such as General MacArthur's proposals to bomb communist bases in China.

Slightly more than 300 Canadian servicemen were killed in action, and 32 were held as prisoners of war and returned after the signing of the armistice.

he would strike a decisive blow against the North Koreans and win the war.

MacArthur had been committed to the idea of the Inchon landing ever since his first inspection tour to Korea back in the dark days of June. By early July MacArthur's staff in Tokyo was hard at work drawing up detailed plans for the landing. MacArthur hoped to launch the invasion by the third week of July, using troops from the First Cavalry Division. But rapid Communist gains made the plan impractical, as the

First was thrown into the defense of the shrinking UN-controlled territory in southernmost Korea. By late July, MacArthur's staff had come up with a new plan for Inchon. This time they would use the marines, the specialists in amphibious landings. The invasion of Inchon, now scheduled for September, would be coordinated with a breakout assault by UN forces from the Pusan Perimeter.

In many ways, Inchon was the worst possible place for MacArthur's amphibious landing. Deep tides and a shallow sea left the harbor at Inchon nothing more than a series of mud flats for much of the day. Moreover, the harbor was guarded by a fortified island that had to be stormed before the main assault could begin. Landing ships could proceed only through a narrow channel in the harbor on a few days of especially high tides. Even on those days, there would be only a few hours in the morning when the tides were right for an assault on the outer island, and then a few hours in the evening when the landing craft could move on to the city's beaches and unload the main assault force. When the marines finally landed in the city in the late afternoon, they would have only about two hours of daylight to secure their positions. If the NKPA proved to be well entrenched in back of the high sea wall that ran along the beach, they would be able to inflict casualties on invaders similar to or worse than those suffered in such bloody World War II assaults as Tarawa and Iwo Jima.

What MacArthur counted on was that the North Koreans, knowing all the disadvantages facing an attacker at Inchon, would let their guard down. But it was a gamble, with potentially disastrous consequences. The Joint Chiefs of Staff (JCS), meeting with MacArthur in Tokyo in early July, were not enthusiastic. A long debate over the wisdom of the attack plan followed. If anyone other than MacArthur had proposed the plan, it would have been dismissed out of hand. But MacArthur's great prestige, as one of the leading commanders of the victorious fighting in the Pacific during World War II, allowed him to win over the critics of the plan. The only alternative, he argued, was a continued bloody battle to defend the Pusan Perimeter.

In August MacArthur was given a reluctant go-ahead by the Joint Chiefs of Staff to prepare for some kind of amphibious landing, though not necessarily at Inchon. MacArthur deliberately kept the JCS in the dark about the final preparations, timing, and place of the invasion, until it was too late to call it off. This was an insult and abuse of authority that the JCS would not forget.

General MacArthur, assisted by Gen. Edward M. Almond (right), observes shelling of Inchon from fleet command ship USS *Mount McKinley*, September 14, 1950. *(National Archives)*

With Walker and the Eighth Army committed to the defense of Pusan, MacArthur decided to form a new unit, the X (Tenth) Corps, to carry out the invasion of Inchon. X Corps was placed under the command of Gen. Edward M. Almond, who had fought bravely in both world wars and had served as MacArthur's chief of staff in the Far East Command. X Corps would function independently of the Eighth Army, with both armies reporting directly to MacArthur in Tokyo. This divided command worked well in the late summer of 1950, but it would cause great problems for the United Nations later in the year.

The strike force for the invasion of Inchon was spearheaded by the U.S. First Marine Division, which included the men of the First Provisional Marine Brigade, already bloodied in the defense of the Pusan Perimeter. They would be backed up by the U.S. Army's Third and Seventh Infantry Divisions, and by South Korean soldiers and marines. This was a huge operation, and preparations for it were hard to conceal. An invasion fleet of 260 ships carrying 70,000 men set sail from Japan,

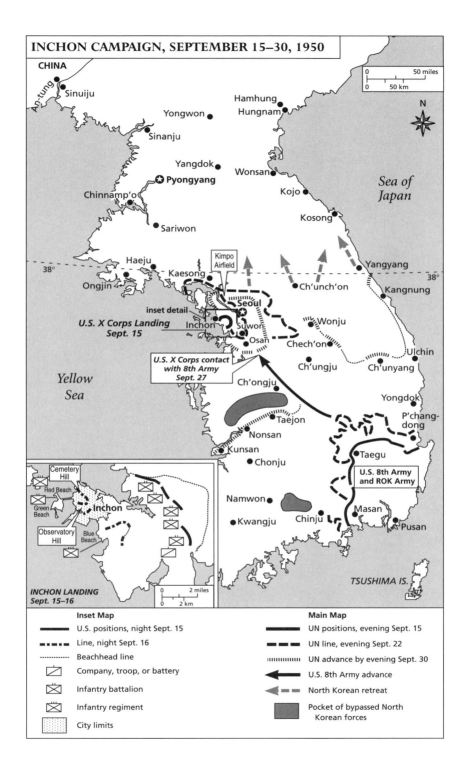

INCHON CAMPAIGN, SEPTEMBER 15–30, 1950

CHINA

An-tung
Sinuiju
Yongwon
Sinanju
Yangdok
Chinnamp'o
Pyongyang
Sariwon

Hamhung
Hungnam
Wonsan
Kojo
Kosong

Sea of Japan

38°

Haeju
Kaesong
Ongjin

Kimpo Airfield

inset detail

Seoul

U.S. X Corps Landing Sept. 15
Inchon
Suwon
Osan

Ch'unch'on
Kangnung
Yangyang

38°

Wonju
Chech'on
Ch'ungju
Ch'unyang
Ulchin

U.S. X Corps contact with 8th Army Sept. 27

Yellow Sea

Ch'ongju

Taejon
Nonsan
Kunsan
Chonju

Yongdok
P'chang-dong

Taegu

U.S. 8th Army and ROK Army

Namwon
Kwangju
Chonju
Chinju
Masan
Pusan

TSUSHIMA IS.

Cemetery Hill
Red Beach
Green Beach
Inchon
Observatory Hill
Blue Beach

INCHON LANDING Sept. 15–16

0   2 miles
0   2 km

Inset Map

———	U.S. positions, night Sept. 15
▬ ▬ ▬	Line, night Sept. 16
··········	Beachhead line
⊡	Company, troop, or battery
⊠	Infantry battalion
⊠	Infantry regiment
▦	City limits

Main Map

———	UN positions, evening Sept. 15
▬ ▬ ▬	UN line, evening Sept. 22
⸽⸽⸽⸽⸽	UN advance by evening Sept. 30
←	U.S. 8th Army advance
▬ ▬ ▬	North Korean retreat
▨	Pocket of bypassed North Korean forces

0   50 miles
0   50 km

N

Korea, and other ports, heading up the western coast of Korea. War correspondents in Japan joked about the launching of "Operation Common Knowledge," while UN planes bombed many potential landing sites along the coast to confuse enemy planners.

The fleet gathered off Inchon on September 14. MacArthur was on board the fleet's command ship, the *Mount McKinley,* to watch the outcome of his great gamble. A heavy naval and air bombardment of the fortified island of Wolmi-do, which lay 500 yards off the main port of Inchon, began at 5:45 A.M. on September 15. The marines hit the beach on Wolmi-do at 6:33 A.M. Some of those taking part in the landings were veterans of the Pacific fighting of World War II, and visions of the bloody reception they had met from the Japanese were going through their minds. But once they landed, they met almost no resistance from the few stunned survivors of the bombardment. The island was reported secured little more than an hour later, with no U.S. deaths. It was a good beginning, and it was followed in the evening by even greater success.

The main landing at Inchon began when high tide came in late that afternoon. The marines hit two beaches, Red Beach in the main port and Blue Beach to the south of the city. They used wooden and aluminum ladders to climb out of landing craft and scale the high concrete seawalls that bordered the city. Marine private Fred Davidson had landed on Wolmi-do early in the morning and spent the day waiting for the main attack to begin. When it came, he had a spectacular view from the top of the 350-foot-high hill on Wolmi-do:

> I could see both landing sites. This was fantastic! It was just like watching a John Wayne movie projected on an enormous 3-D Cinemascope screen. Not everyone can say they actually witnessed a Marine Division making a landing on a beach. It was simply beautiful!

The operation was not without some hitches. The navy did not always get the marines on the right beaches at the right time. Marine major Edwin Simmons was searching for his assigned landing zone through the smoke drifting off Blue Beach. He asked the driver of his LVT (landing vehicle tank) if he had a compass. "He looked at his instrument panel and said, 'Search me. Six weeks ago I was driving a truck in San Francisco.'" Once ashore, Americans were in more danger from the navy's "friendly fire" than they were from the light resistance

Over the top: Marines hit the beach at Inchon, September 15, 1950.
(National Archives)

put up by the North Koreans. Despite such mishaps, the marines had secured the city by midnight at a cost of only 20 men killed. One of the few who died that day was a marine lieutenant named Baldomero "Punchy" Lopez. Lopez had been one of the first marines over the sea-wall at Red Beach. Attacking a North Korean bunker, he was shot in the hand and had to drop the grenade he was holding. In order to protect the other men in his platoon he threw himself on top of the loose grenade and was killed in the explosion. He was posthumously awarded the Congressional Medal of Honor for his heroism.

Eighteen thousand Americans were ashore at Inchon before the night ended. Fifty thousand were ashore within the next four days. By the end of the first full day of the invasion, the marines had advanced 10 miles eastward on the road to Seoul. MacArthur himself was ashore on September 17, driving to the front to see the remains of a convoy of North Korean tanks the marines had just destroyed.

The North Koreans, while taken by surprise, were not yet defeated. They put up a stiff fight in the streets of Seoul in the last week of

The Inchon landing, September 15, 1950 *(National Archives)*

September. General Almond declared the city of Seoul officially "liberated" on September 25, three months to the day after the start of the North Korean invasion. In fact, it took another three days of heavy fighting in the center of the city to clear out enemy resistance. The North Koreans had built roadblocks in the streets that had to be cleared with bulldozers before U.S. tanks could move ahead, while hidden snipers picked off U.S. infantrymen. The Americans advanced slowly through the city, fighting building by building and street by street. Much of the city was leveled, and many civilians were killed in the battle. On September 29, with artillery fire still shaking the city, General MacArthur turned over the liberated South Korean capital in the name of the United Nations and "a merciful Providence" to a tearful Syngman Rhee.

While X Corps was breaking out of Inchon, the Eighth Army was breaking out of the Pusan Perimeter. On September 16, Walker's men launched coordinated assaults all along the perimeter. After three days of hard fighting, the NKPA were retreating all along the line. Walker's Eighth Army linked up with Almond's X Corps on September 27 near the site of the original U.S. defeat at Osan. And South Korean soldiers reached the 38th parallel two days later.

With the success of the Inchon invasion and the breakout from Pusan, the United States and the United Nations had achieved all of the goals outlined in the Security Council resolutions of the early summer. The cost of victory had been high. Total U.S. casualties at the end of September 1950 included 6,000 dead, 19,000 wounded, and 2,500 captured or missing. But South Korea was freed from its invaders, who were driven back in disorder into North Korea. Collective security had triumphed over aggression.

The rapid and overwhelming nature of victory in September 1950 bred a fatal arrogance among the victors that led to a redefinition of war aims. In Tokyo and Washington, U.S. leaders now saw what they believed was a golden opportunity to "roll back" communism by continuing the UN drive into North Korea. This decision prolonged the

Marines fight house to house to rid Seoul of its North Korean occupiers in late September 1950. Seoul would change hands four times in the course of the war. *(U.S. Army Military History Institute)*

On September 29, 1950, Seoul was liberated, and the flag was raised over the U.S. consulate. *(National Archives)*

war for an additional two years during which tens of thousands more Americans and millions of Koreans would lose their lives. The tremendous UN military victory in the late summer of 1950 prepared the way for military disaster in the fall and winter to come.

5

DISASTER IN
THE NORTH

Between June and September 1950 communism had been dealt a major defeat in Korea. Thanks to the swift intervention of the United Nations, South Korean independence had been maintained and the principle of collective security against external aggression strengthened. But the war did not come to an end when UN forces drove the North Koreans back across the border. Even before the Inchon invasion turned the tide of battle in South Korea, U.S. policy makers were debating whether or not UN armies should cross the 38th parallel into North Korea. On September 27, the Joint Chiefs of Staff sent MacArthur a directive authorizing him to carry the war to the north. The U.S. government deliberately kept hazy the purpose for the invasion of the north. While the Americans wanted to see all of Korea united under the anticommunist government of Syngman Rhee, some of their UN allies were reluctant to discard the original, purely defensive justification for intervention. As far as the world was told, Americans and other UN forces were crossing the border simply to complete the destruction of the North Korean army's offensive capacity.

Despite the smashing victory U.S. troops had already gained, President Truman was fearful of the domestic political consequences of appearing "soft on communism" should the UN offensive be halted short of total victory. Public opinion polls revealed that a majority of Americans would view any plan to halt the UN offensive at the 38th parallel as "appeasement" of the Communists. Only five years earlier, General MacArthur had accepted the unconditional surrender of the Japanese aboard a U.S. warship in Tokyo Bay. The lesson of the two world wars the United States had fought in the 20th century seemed clear: Total victory over an aggressor was the only sure guarantee against future aggression. This view had an extremely popular spokesman in Douglas MacArthur, whose prestige was at an all-time high after his triumph at Inchon. Now, he assured the president and the Joint Chiefs of Staff complete victory in Korea was within the grasp of the United States at little or no risk of a wider or prolonged war. How could they refuse?

Whatever the United Nations decided to do, Syngman Rhee was determined to have his armies conquer North Korea, now that his life-long ambition of ruling a united Korea seemed so close to being realized. The ROKs began their advance up the eastern coast of North Korea on October 1. They made it look easy. By October 10, ROK units had entered the port city of Wonsan, 110 miles north of the border, and were making impressive gains in the middle of the peninsula as well. The battered NKPA was incapable of mounting a sustained resistance to the invaders. By the third week of October, advanced ROK units were approaching the Yalu River.

On October 9, U.S. forces crossed the 38th parallel, joining the ROK offensive against North Korea. Over the objections of many of his senior commanders in Korea, MacArthur divided his forces in a two-pronged drive northward. North Korea's mountainous central region made a coordinated assault alongside a wide front impossible. MacArthur decided that the Eighth Army, under the command of Gen. Walton Walker, should push northward from Seoul along the highway and railroad line linking the South Korean capital to the North Korean capital of Pyongyang. Meanwhile, MacArthur dispatched X Corps, the victors of Inchon, on a long, slow boat trip all the way around the Korean Peninsula to the eastern coast of North Korea. At a moment when the enemy was falling back in disorder, his choice of strategy defied military common sense. But MacArthur had grown enamored of amphibious landings, which had produced such a resounding victory at Inchon. He wanted to repeat the tactic, landing X Corps at the North Korean port of Wonsan. From there, X Corps, under the command of Gen. Edward Almond, would be in a position to advance westward to link up with the Eighth Army at Pyongyang.

Getting X Corps on board ship at Inchon and off again at Wonsan proved a logistical nightmare, wasting precious weeks. The landing at Wonsan was stripped of any real strategic value when the ROKs, march-

Crossing the 38th parallel *(National Archives)*

ing by land, captured the city on October 10. Complicating matters even further, it took the U.S. Navy two weeks to sweep Wonsan Harbor clean of the mines sown by the North Koreans, while the bored marines (who began to call the plan "Operation Yo Yo") waited uselessly off shore. By the time X Corps finally landed on October 25, its mission had changed. Pyongyang had already fallen to the hard-charging Eighth Army. MacArthur now ordered that X Corps (reinforced by soldiers from the Seventh Division, who landed unopposed at the North Korean port of Iwon on October 29, and later by the army's Third Division) drive northward toward the Yalu, linking up with the Eighth Army north of the central mountainous region of the country.

UN forces in eastern North Korea pushed inland without great difficulty. The marines, along with units from the army Seventh Infantry Division, advanced 64 miles along the road north from the port of Hungnam to the village of Hagaru, at the bottom of the Chosin Reservoir. (The reservoir had been built by the Japanese as part of northern Korea's hydroelectric system.) From there, U.S. soldiers advanced up the eastern shore, while the marines headed northwest of the reservoir toward the Yalu River.

By late October the United Nations had two separate armies in North Korea, under separate command, acting independently and unable to maintain any ground contact with each other. The Eighth Army and X Corps were in a race to penetrate North Korea. But in between the two northward-driving UN armies lay a 75-mile-wide expanse of roadless and unguarded mountains. It was almost a textbook illustration of a fundamental military error—dividing forces and exposing vulnerable flanks in the face of the enemy. As long as the only foe the UN forces had to face was the crumbling NKPA, it did not make a great deal of difference. But there were disturbing signs that this was about to change.

U.S. policy-making in the Korean War was complicated by tensions building between the commander in chief, President Truman, and the commander of UN forces in Korea, General MacArthur. By midsummer of 1950, differences between MacArthur and Truman had already been publicly revealed. On his own initiative, MacArthur made a trip to Taiwan in late July to shore up Nationalist Chinese morale at a moment when an invasion by Chinese Communists seemed imminent. In a press conference following his meeting with Chinese Nationalist leader Chiang Kai-shek, MacArthur implied that the United States was prepared to come to the aid of Chiang's regime in the event of a Communist Chinese invasion attempt. Chiang went even further, declaring that the United States and Nationalist Chinese were prepared to work together for "final victory" over the Chinese Communists, a statement that could be interpreted to mean that the United States was prepared to back Chiang in a Nationalist invasion of the mainland.

Truman, who had no intention of committing the U.S. military to the invasion of China, was infuriated by these comments. The president feared that such loose talk increased the likelihood of Chinese intervention in the Korean conflict. (For the same reason, he had already turned down Chiang Kai-shek's offer to send 30,000 Nationalist Chinese troops to fight in South Korea.) There was also an important constitutional issue involved. MacArthur, as the regional military commander, seemed to be challenging the right of elected civilian authorities to determine U.S. foreign policy.

Truman still hoped that these differences could be reconciled. He dispatched his National Security Advisor, Averell Harriman, to Tokyo to make it clear to MacArthur who was in charge. MacArthur told Harriman that he would "as a soldier, obey any orders that he received from the President." Harriman was not reassured. As he reported to Truman

"Two Chinas" Confront Each Other

THE COMMUNIST-CONTROLLED PEOPLE'S REPUBLIC OF China had not yet marked its ninth month of existence when war broke out between the two Koreas. While Mao Zedong was preoccupied in 1949–50 with consolidating Communist control of the mainland, he had not forgotten that his longtime enemy, Nationalist leader Chiang Kai-shek, still ruled over the Chinese province of Taiwan with the aid of 2 million anticommunist Chinese who had fled with him to refuge on the island. From this bastion, Chiang repeatedly announced his intention of returning to the mainland someday to drive out the Communists. Had the North Koreans prevailed in their conquest of South Korea, without interference from the United States, Mao would have been encouraged on his designs on Taiwan. But, as events turned out, the Korean War proved Chiang's salvation. With the U.S. Seventh Fleet patrolling the Straits of Taiwan, the Chinese Communists lost the opportunity to complete their conquest. "Two Chinas" would confront each other across the straits for decades to come.

later, "I did not feel that we came to a full agreement" about U.S. policy toward Nationalist China. MacArthur "accepted the President's position and will act accordingly, but without full conviction."

The fragile truce between Truman and MacArthur did not last long. At the end of August MacArthur drafted a letter to be read to the annual convention of the Veterans of Foreign Wars (VFW), in which he described Taiwan as the key to the defense of all U.S. interests in the Pacific. Given their previous disagreement, Truman regarded this as another act of insubordination by MacArthur and considered removing him from command. But with the landings at Inchon scheduled to take place in only three weeks, Truman did not want to do anything to risk the success of the operation. Instead he sent MacArthur a cable demanding that he retract his statement on Taiwan. MacArthur complied, though not before the contents of the VFW letter were leaked to the U.S. press.

Truman had good reason to be concerned about the intentions of Communist China's leader, Mao Zedong. Mao, whose victorious armies had secured communist power only a year before, had no intention of allowing a hostile power to take over a country on China's border. Korea, after all, had been one of the bases from which the Japanese had attacked and conquered Manchuria in the 1930s. The Chinese government began sending out diplomatic signals as early as August that it would not tolerate a U.S./UN invasion of North Korea. On September 30, after Seoul had been recaptured, but before UN forces crossed the 38th parallel, Chinese foreign minister Zhou Enlai (Chou En-lai) warned in a speech in Peking that "The Chinese people enthusiastically love peace, but [will not] tolerate seeing their neighbors being savagely invaded by the imperialists." A few days later Chou bluntly warned the Indian ambassador to China that if the Americans crossed the 38th parallel, the Chinese would send their troops south across the Yalu. The United States chose to disregard these warnings, and that proved to be a mistake.

Two weeks after Chou's warning to the Indian ambassador, and a week after the Eighth Army crossed the 38th parallel, Chinese Communist soldiers began their move into North Korea under cover of

Mao Zedong (1893–1976), chairman of the Chinese Communist Party
(New York Public Library)

President Truman
meets with General
MacArthur on Wake
Island and awards him
the Distinguished
Service Medal, as U.S.
Ambassador to Korea
John Muccio looks on,
October 15, 1950.
*(Lyndon Baines Johnson
Library & Museum)*

darkness. By October 24, nearly 200,000 Chinese soldiers, undetected by U.S. intelligence, had already crossed the river and were hiding in the rugged northern provinces of North Korea. Many more were on the way. In U.S. military lingo, these units were referred to as the Chinese Communist Forces (CCF). The Chinese government would maintain that these were "volunteers," but in fact they were regular, battle-hardened units of the Chinese People's Liberation Army. The Chinese kept the names of the units and their commanders a secret. Some historians believe that Lin Biao (Piao), a leading Chinese Communist with considerable military experience, initially commanded the Chinese forces committed to Korea. By 1951 command had shifted to Gen. Peng Dehuai (P'eng Teh-huai), a heavyset man of peasant background who was a rugged and aggressive commander. Like the men under their command, Lin and Peng had gained a wealth of battlefield experience fighting against the Japanese and the Chinese Nationalists.

While the Chinese secretly moved into North Korea, Truman flew to Wake Island in the mid-Pacific for a meeting on October 15 with

MacArthur. Although the meeting was apparently cordial, the two leaders came away from it despising each other. MacArthur regarded the entire affair, which had been Truman's idea, as a publicity stunt to aid the Democrats' chances in the upcoming congressional elections in November. For his part, Truman was repelled by MacArthur's evident sense of self-importance. Truman may have had the elections in mind when he scheduled the meeting, but he also wanted MacArthur's assurance that the invasion of North Korea would not lead to Chinese intervention. MacArthur replied that there was "very little" chance of that happening, and even if the Chinese did decide to cross the Yalu River, the U.S. air force would "slaughter" them.

When UN forces first moved into North Korea, their orders expressly prohibited them from approaching the country's border provinces with China or the Soviet Union. Only ROK forces would be allowed to pursue the enemy that far northward, to avoid possible clashes between U.S. troops and those of the communist giants to the north. But again, with easy victory in sight, MacArthur decided to stretch his authority. On October 24, without consulting the military Joint Chiefs of Staff (JCS) in Washington, he ordered UN commanders "to drive forward through the north with all speed and with full utilization of their forces." The JCS was disturbed by the order, but once again did not restrain MacArthur.

In the summer fighting in South Korea, U.S. troops had suffered from the brutal heat. Now the Americans fighting in North Korea were beginning to suffer from the onset of the bitter winter cold. Many of them had not been issued heavy winter clothing, and they longed for a warm, dry, comfortable barracks back in the United States or Japan. Still, with the NKPA soldiers fleeing before them, Americans were confident that the worst was past them. After all, General MacArthur had declared that the troops would be "home by Christmas." Pvt. James Cardinal of the Fifth Cavalry Regiment wrote his parents after taking part in the capture of Pyongyang: "There's a rumor going around that the 1st Cavalry Division is returning to Japan pretty soon, now that the war is over. I certainly hope so. I'm sick of this country and this war." Some soldiers were so confident that they even abandoned their heavy steel helmets in the belief that they would not see any more combat.

But it soon became apparent that such confidence was misplaced. The war was not over by a long shot. The first clash between the advancing UN forces and the CCF came on October 26. An ROK battalion that

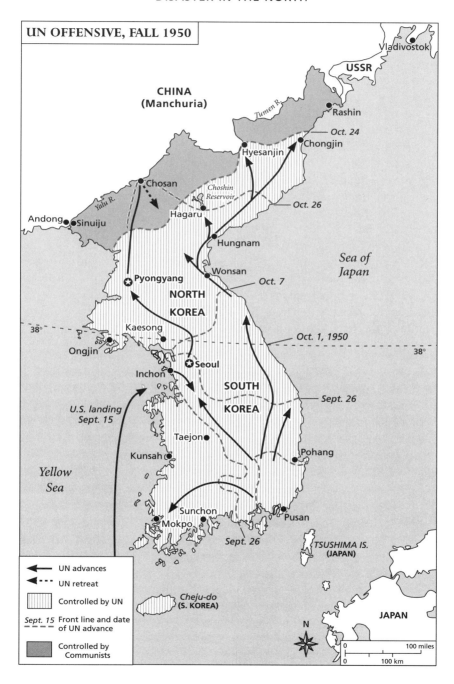

UN OFFENSIVE, FALL 1950

Vladivostok

USSR

CHINA
(Manchuria)

Tumen R.

Rashin

Oct. 24
Chongjin

Hyesanjin

Chosan

Choshin
Reservoir

Oct. 26

Yalu R.

Andong Sinuiju

Hagaru

Hungnam

Sea of
Japan

Wonsan

Oct. 7

Pyongyang

NORTH

KOREA

Kaesong

Oct. 1, 1950

38°

Ongjin

38°

Inchon

Seoul

SOUTH

U.S. landing
Sept. 15

KOREA

Sept. 26

Taejon

Kunsah

Pohang

Yellow
Sea

Sunchon

Pusan

Mokpo

Sept. 26

TSUSHIMA IS.
(JAPAN)

UN advances

UN retreat

Controlled by UN

Cheju-do
(S. KOREA)

JAPAN

Sept. 15 Front line and date
of UN advance

Controlled by
Communists

N

0   100 miles

0   100 km

had reached a position about 40 miles south of the Yalu was set upon by the Chinese and destroyed. Other ROK units were hammered in the week that followed. Despite the fact that some Chinese soldiers had been captured in the fighting, MacArthur at first refused to believe that the CCF was involved at all. Finally convinced that there were Chinese in North Korea, he suggested that the communists had sent in only a token force of fewer than 20,000 troops.

The first CCF attack on U.S. troops came on November 1. Chinese soldiers attacked the Eighth U.S. Cavalry, which was occupying the town of Unsan. The attack came as a total surprise. The Chinese cut off the Americans' line of retreat and inflicted heavy casualties in fierce hand-to-hand combat. Chinese soldiers, with bugles and whistles blowing, swarmed over U.S. defenses. The Fifth Cavalry, which tried unsuccessfully to break through to relieve the encircled Eighth, was also hard hit. Capt. Norman Allen of the Fifth Cavalry wrote home to his mother shortly after the battle at Unsan, "Anyone who says they aren't [Chinese] is crazy!" The next day marines near the Chosin Reservoir engaged the Chinese but fared better than the Eighth Army's soldiers. The marines beat back the CCF attackers and were able to continue their advance.

The Russian-built MiG-15 fighter interceptor that was flown to a U.S. Air Force base in Kimpo near Seoul on September 21, 1953, by a North Korean officer pilot in a daring flight to freedom *(National Archives)*

F-86 Sabre jets were the MiG killers of the war. *(U.S. Army Center of Military History)*

In another ominous development, Chinese MiG-15 fighter planes began to challenge UN control of the air south of the Yalu in early November. The first U.S. plane was downed by a MiG on November 8. U.S. pilots dubbed the area just south of the Yalu "MiG alley" and were angered that they were not allowed to follow the MiGs in hot pursuit when Chinese pilots flew back across the Yalu to sanctuary in Manchuria. But the British—members of the UN team that was nominally in charge of the war—insisted that there be no hot pursuit; they feared any action that might provoke a full-scale Chinese intervention, and Washington went along. The Chinese, for their part, avoided direct attacks on UN military ground forces from the air.

MacArthur, finally convinced of the reality of Chinese intervention, ordered U.S. planes to bomb the bridges across the Yalu linking Manchuria and North Korea. Truman, hearing of the order and fearing the consequences of accidental bombing of Chinese territory, at first countermanded it. But after MacArthur warned of a "calamity of major proportion" unless the bridges were bombed, Truman relented. It made no difference, because the bombers were unable to destroy all the bridges, and in mid-November the Yalu froze solid, allowing troops and supplies to cross without the use of bridges.

The JCS were having increasing doubts about MacArthur's plans for victory. They questioned whether the United States should shift its strategy, halt its military offensive, and seek a political settlement to the conflict. MacArthur, responding on November 9, still insisted that he could destroy any forces the Chinese were prepared to commit to the war. He now planned to launch an offensive in late November to bring the war to "complete victory."

Having given the UN forces a bloody nose, the CCF suddenly halted their attacks and withdrew to their hidden positions on November 7. MacArthur, who still underestimated the number of Chinese troops in the country, was once again lulled into overconfidence. The Eighth Army, which had pulled back to more defensible positions after the first Chinese attacks, resumed its advance in the second week of November.

On November 23, Thanksgiving Day, UN troops in Korea ate a special turkey dinner, flown or trucked up to the front. It was, Pvt. Arthur Cohen of the army's Second Division wrote in his diary, "the best meal we had in Korea." Some of the soldiers at the front even enjoyed the luxury of hot showers and a change of clothes. On the next day, November 24, UN forces renewed their offensive, prepared to win the war and be home for Christmas. Already a small unit from the army's Seventh U.S. Division had reached the Yalu River at Hyesanjin. Pvt. Paul Martin of the First Marine Division remembered that "the sweet smell of victory was again in the air." That was when disaster struck. Army historian Roy Appleman would later write that in the month that followed Thanksgiving 1950, "a series of disasters unequaled in our country's history overwhelmed American arms."

The second phase of the Chinese offensive was about to begin. The Chinese, who lacked tanks, air support, and heavy artillery, relied instead on surprise to defeat the Americans. CCF commanders displayed an extraordinary ability to move large numbers of troops on night marches undetected through difficult terrain. Chinese troops were masters of the art of camouflage and could stay completely hidden during the day. The official U.S. Marine Corps history of the war noted: "The Chinese coolie in the padded cotton uniform could do one thing better than any other soldier on earth; he could infiltrate around an enemy position in the darkness with unbelievable stealth." While newspapers in the United States carried sensational dispatches about Chinese "human wave" attacks, the reality at the front was quite different. As marine historians noted, "The Chinese seldom attacked in units larger than a regiment . . . It was not mass but deception and surprise which made the Chinese Red formidable." Despite limited food, inadequate clothing, and few other comforts, the Chinese soldiers proved tough, disciplined fighters, not the "laundry-men" that MacArthur ridiculed.

The gathering storm broke on the evening of November 25, when the Eighth Army was hit with "human wave" assaults. It proved a terrifying experience for the U.S. soldiers. Many units were overrun. Lt. Ellison Wynn of the Ninth Infantry held out with his troops against overwhelming odds. When he ran out of ammunition, he began hurling rocks and cans of field rations at the enemy, until he was wounded by an enemy grenade. (Wynn miraculously survived the attack and was awarded a Distinguished Service Cross for heroism.) Overall, the Eighth Army's exposed front line disintegrated into chaos. The army's Second Division, Twenty-fifth Division, and First Cavalry Division all took heavy losses in the Chinese attacks, as did three ROK divisions and the Turkish Brigade. MacArthur, finally conceding the dangers his troops

The 937th Field Artillery's self-propelled 155 mm "Long Tom" guns light up the sky with a nighttime barrage. *(U.S. Army Military History Institute)*

The U.S. Air Force in the Korean War

THE KOREAN WAR REPRESENTED A NEW STAGE IN THE history of U.S. air power. It was the first war in which the U.S. Air Force (USAF) fought as a separate branch of the armed services. It was also the first war in which jet-propelled aircraft played a major role in aerial warfare. While the United States suffered major setbacks on the ground in the summer of 1950, and again between November 1950 and March 1951, it established its air superiority in the first days of the war and thereafter never lost control of the skies.

The USAF's Far East Air Force, which consisted of the Fifth Air Force (used for tactical operations), Bomber Command, and Combat Cargo Command, flew nearly 750,000 sorties during the war. By the end of the war, USAF pilots were credited with shooting down 950 enemy aircraft, destroying more than 1,300 tanks, and killing nearly 185,000 enemy troops.

The best-known plane flown by USAF fighter pilots during the Korean War was the F-86 Sabre jet, which racked up an impressive eight-to-one kill ratio over the skies of North Korea in combat with communist jets. There were 38 air force pilots in the Korean War who won ace status (credited with shooting down five or more enemy aircraft).

More than 1,400 USAF aircraft of all types were downed by enemy fire or other causes during the war; 1,180 USAF personnel were killed in action; many thousands more were listed as missing in action and presumed to have been killed. Two hundred and fourteen airmen returned from prisoner-of-war camps at the end of the war, and an undetermined number of others died in captivity.

faced, cabled the Pentagon on November 28: "We face an entirely new war." The arrival of MacArthur's cable, so different from the assurances he had given Truman six weeks earlier at Wake Island, shocked officials in Washington.

The Eighth Army was forced to fall back. General Walker had originally hoped to hold Pyongyang against the Chinese offensive, but soon decided to abandon all of North Korea. Pyongyang was evacuated by December5, its huge supply dumps set on fire and hundreds of vehicles abandoned by the retreating Americans. By December 13, the Eighth Army had taken up new defensive lines south of the 38th parallel. They were back to where they had started in October.

However disorganized and disheartening the Eighth Army's retreat, it was nothing compared to the plight of the marines and soldiers of X Corps to the east. For a month, General Almond had been pressing his field commanders to advance as rapidly as possible, hoping to beat the Eighth Army to the Yalu. On November 27, two days after the start of a massive CCF assault on the Eighth Army, Almond ordered the marines on the west side of the Chosin Reservoir and the army's Seventh Division on the east side of the reservoir to renew their offensive. Many officers, especially the marines' battle-hardened commander Gen. Oliver P. Smith, were reluctant to advance any farther, without knowing the extent of the CCF presence. The marines' supply line from the port of Hungnam was already stretched out and vulnerable to attack at many points. The farther the marines advanced up the western side of the Chosin Reservoir, the greater the risk they ran of being cut off by the enemy.

The Chinese struck X Corps on the night of November 27. More than 100,000 CCF troops had taken up positions in the hills overlooking the road that was the X Corps lifeline to Hungnam. On the east side of the Chosin Reservoir, the 3,200 soldiers of Task Force MacLean (named for its commander, Col. Allan D. "Mac" MacLean) found themselves cut off by the Chinese from any retreat. For the next four days they fought a desperate battle to break through Chinese roadblocks. MacLean was wounded and captured by the Chinese, dying a few days later in captivity. His successor, Lt. Col. Don C. Faith, was killed and posthumously awarded the Medal of Honor. The column of trucks carrying the unit's wounded soldiers was mistakenly hit with napalm by U.S. aircraft. In the end, only about 1,000 of the task force's 3,200 men escaped death or capture, and only about 350 of these were in any condition to fight. The pitiful remnants of the task force staggered or dragged themselves across the frozen waters of the Chosin to the marine stronghold at Hagaru on the reservoir's southern tip.

The same fate threatened to overtake the 10,000 marines of the First Marine Division, about 2,000 U.S. soldiers, and a small unit of British Royal Marine Commandos on the western side of the reservoir. In an epic battle, starting on December 1, these men fought their way through the encircling Chinese army back to the coast. The battle of the Chosin Reservoir was destined to become the most famous battle of the

Marines withdraw to Hagaru, November 28–December 3, 1950, in five days and nights of below-zero winds and icy roads. *(National Archives)*

Korean War. The fact that the marines and others made it out had much to do with the determination and the foresight of their commander, Gen. Oliver P. Smith. Before the Chinese attack, Smith had advanced cautiously, carefully stockpiling supplies along the road from Hungnam. When he began his retreat, he resisted suggestions that his men abandon their vehicles and be evacuated by plane from Hagaru. Smith reasoned that even if some of his men could be evacuated by air, the Chinese would soon be able to overrun the positions of those who guarded the airstrip's shrinking perimeter. In the end, the only Americans to be flown out of Hagaru were 4,000 wounded men. The rest would have to walk to the sea. Smith shared the sufferings of his men in the bitter cold. His attitude was summed up in a famous remark he made on December 4, when he responded to a question from a war correspondent about the marines' "retreat": "We're not retreating. We are just advancing in a different direction."

By December 4, all the surviving Americans had made it back to Hagaru. Marine private Doug Michaud would recall later:

> All the way from Yudam-ni to Hagaru-ri it was, "Five more miles, guys, warm buildings, hot chow. Just five miles guys." . . . Hell, I thought, the war's over at Hagaru-ri. No one suspected that it would get worse there.

From Hagaru, starting on December 6, the Americans fought their way off the plateau and down a long mountain road to the valley leading to Hungnam. By December 7, all the UN forces were out of Hagaru, and the rear guard blew up the bridge over the Changjun River south of the town to slow the Chinese following. But the road ahead was full of peril. It was hard and treacherous, every step of the way. Riding down the narrow, icy, twisting road, trucks and tanks skidded off onto the rocks below. The Chinese held the hills and seemed to lie in ambush around each new bend in the road. Somehow the exhausted Americans found the strength to fight on. Air strikes helped beat back the attacks, and supplies were parachuted in to the long column of trucks and marching men. But nothing could protect the men from the freezing cold. At night, temperatures dropped to 20 degrees below zero. A frozen weapon could cost a man his life, so the marines slept with their rifles pressed against their bodies. Cans of emergency rations and canteens of water had to be thawed over open fires so that the men could eat and drink. A lucky soldier or marine was able to take a turn thawing out in a "warming tent," heated by little stoves, before being sent back to an icy foxhole or to trudge on down the road. Lives of wounded men were lost because doctors could not use blood plasma, which froze in the bottles and tubes. Frostbitten hands and feet were a constant danger. Marine private Jack Wright was ordered onto a truck when his feet froze. An older marine on the truck told Wright to take off his boot.

> When I pulled the socks off, a layer of skin also came off. The old guy unbuttoned his parka and dungaree jacket and took my foot and placed it on his bare belly. That's how one Marine will take care of another . . .

The Chinese also suffered in the intense cold. Marine sergeant Lee Bergee captured "several exhausted Chinese" wearing lightweight tennis shoes and whose feet had swollen to "the size of footballs" from the effects of frostbite. "Some of them," he remembered, "had to have their fingers broken in order for us to take the rifles from their frozen hands."

To cut off the U.S. retreat, the Chinese had blown a 16-foot gap in a bridge that spanned the road at a place known as Funchilin Pass. The surrounding hillsides were so steep that there was no way for trucks or tanks to bypass the bridge. But U.S. engineers were able to bridge the gap with heavy steel spans dropped by parachute from the air. When the last American had crossed the bridge on December 11, the engineers blew up the bridge. That same day, the last of the weary marines reached safety within the U.S. Army's perimeter around Hungnam. Master Sgt. Thomas Britt of the army's Third Division was part of a task force sent out from Hungnam to link up with the marines:

> Cold chills still go up my spine as I recall watching Marines, themselves frozen from head to foot, meticulously caring for their wounded and bringing back the dead bodies of their comrades. The Marines were battle-scarred, but still looked as if they could do battle. It reminded me of pictures I've seen of General Washington's frozen troops at Valley Forge.

In the week before Christmas, 22,000 marines, 80,000 other troops, and 90,000 refugees were evacuated by sea from the port of Hungnam, which was then destroyed by naval gunfire. The marines lost more than

In December 1950, marines gather their dead for burial after an ambush during the withdrawal from Chosin Reservoir. *(Lyndon Baines Johnson Library & Museum)*

DISASTER IN THE NORTH

A column of Korean civilian refugees moves south before advancing
Chinese armies, January 1951. *(U.S. Army Military History Institute)*

700 killed, nearly 200 missing, and 3,500 wounded in the withdrawal
from the Chosin Reservoir. Thousands more were struck down by frostbite or dysentery. More than 10,000 Chinese attackers were killed.

On the home front Americans had closely followed the reports of
the Chosin Reservoir battle and were cheered by the marines' heroic
effort to reach Hungnam. But there was little else to cheer about in the
news from Korea. By Christmas 1950, Korea had seen yet another great
reversal in the fortunes of war, the third since the North Korean invasion in June. The Eighth Army and X Corps had abandoned North
Korea. To top off a month of bad news, the commander of the Eighth
Army, Gen. Walton Walker, was killed in an accident on December 23,
when the jeep he was traveling in swerved into a ditch to avoid a colli-
sion with an ROK weapons carrier.

Extreme pessimism once again became the mood in Washington. It
was feared that the Chinese might continue their advance and overrun
the U.S. forces in South Korea. At a press conference on November 30,
Truman made headlines (and shocked his British allies, who had not
been consulted) by threatening to use atomic weapons in Korea if
needed. Contingency plans were drawn up for a withdrawal back to the
Pusan Perimeter, and even for a total evacuation. General MacArthur
argued that the United States should be prepared to fight all-out war to

Sounding "Taps" over the graves of fallen Leathernecks during memorial services at the First Marine Division cemetery at Hungnam, following the division's heroic breakout from Chosin Reservoir, December 13, 1950
(National Archives/DOD, War & Conflict, #1513)

salvage its position in Korea, even at the risk of involving the Soviet Union and China in a world war. He demanded that UN forces be reinforced with Chinese Nationalist troops, that the U.S. navy blockade the Chinese coasts, and that the U.S. Air Force bomb Manchuria. Despite his careless talk about atomic weapons, Truman wanted to limit the size of the conflict. He feared, however, that the war would spread regardless of his intentions, confiding to his diary on December 9 that it seemed "like World War III is here."

But the conflict remained a localized and limited war. For the next two years U.S. leaders searched for a way to bring the war to an end. All the while, the killing continued. From now on it would be a war to hold the line, until the diplomats could patch up some kind of mutually acceptable peace.

6

RIDGWAY TAKES COMMAND

The two months that followed the launching of the Chinese offensive in November 1950 saw the longest retreat in U.S. military history. Before a secure defensive line was established (very near Osan, where Task Force Smith had first met the North Koreans the previous July), the U.S. Eighth Army had retreated 275 miles from the positions it held on the eve of the Chinese attack. North Korea was once again entirely under Communist control, and South Korea's future looked grim. But with the arrival of a new commander, Gen. Matthew Ridgway, the Eighth Army regained its fighting spirit. And with the relief of General MacArthur as UN supreme commander, President Truman reestablished his control over foreign policy and military decision making in the Korean War. By the late spring of 1951 it was evident that the Communists would not be able to drive the UN forces out of South Korea. But no one knew how long it would be before a negotiated settlement could end the bloody stalemate on the battlefield.

As 1950 drew to an end, many U.S. troops were left demoralized by the ferocity of the Chinese attacks. "Bug-out fever" infected the UN forces. Pfc. James Cardinal of the Fifth Cavalry wrote to his parents on January 7, 1951: "It looks like the beginning of the end. The Chinese are kicking hell out of the U.S. Army, and I think we are getting out, at least I hope so . . . I don't think we can hold the Chinks." But even as Cardinal wrote his letter, the battlefield advantage in Korea began to shift to the UN.

Gen. Matthew B.
Ridgway, newly
appointed Eighth U.S.
Army commander
*(Lyndon Baines Johnson
Library & Museum)*

Like MacArthur after Inchon, Chinese leaders deluded themselves into believing that a total, smashing victory would soon be theirs. Rather than halting their advance at the 38th parallel, they pressed on with their offensive. The United Nations made several proposals for a cease-fire to the Chinese. In January 1951 the United Nations proposed that an international conference be held after the establishment of a cease-fire in Korea; the conference could discuss such issues as Chinese membership in the United Nations and the future of Taiwan. (Chiang Kai-shek's government still held the Chinese seat in the UN Security Council.) But Chinese Communist leaders were not interested. In the face of Communist recalcitrance, the United States was able to win a vote of the UN General Assembly on February 1, branding the Chinese aggressors for their intervention in Korea. Like the Americans in the fall of 1950, the Chinese leaders would pay heavily for their delusions in the spring of 1951.

Chinese advantages slipped away in January. They had suffered heavy losses in their offensive in December. And the farther south they advanced, the more difficult it was for them to keep their remaining

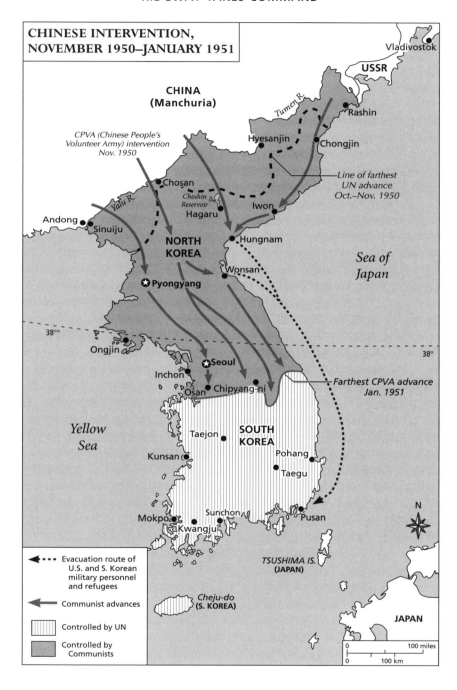

**CHINESE INTERVENTION,
NOVEMBER 1950–JANUARY 1951**

troops supplied. UN forces, for their part, were now closer to their own supply depots and ports and fighting on more favorable terrain. Instead of having two armies separated by a vast expanse of roadless terrain, as they did in North Korea, the UN forces were united in a single force. (After the withdrawal from North Korea, X Corps was no longer treated as a separate army but came under the direction of the Eighth Army commander.) For the first time in the war, the United Nations could maintain a more or less continuous defensive line across the Korean Peninsula, shifting forces as needed by rail or road along the battlefront. And the Eighth Army gained a competent and charismatic leader who was determined to restore the morale and fighting capabilities of the hard-pressed U.S. soldiers.

Lt. Gen. Matthew Ridgway had a long and distinguished military career behind him when he arrived in Korea on December 26. The 56-year-old Ridgway had been serving in Washington, D.C., as the army's deputy chief of staff for administration. But he was not a desk-bound soldier. A graduate of West Point in 1917, he had been given command of the Eighty-second Airborne Division in World War II and had parachuted with his men behind enemy lines in the invasion of Sicily in 1943 and the invasion of Normandy in 1944. Ridgway had the respect of the Joint Chiefs of Staff in Washington and of General MacArthur. Truman and the Joint Chiefs expected that, unlike his predecessor, General Walker, Ridgway would be able to play a more independent role in shaping Korean strategy. When Ridgway met with MacArthur in Tokyo on December 26, MacArthur told him, "The Eighth Army is yours, Matt. Do what you think best."

Ridgway had only just arrived in Korea when the Chinese launched their Third Phase Offensive on New Year's Eve. The Eighth Army, which had taken up positions near the 38th parallel, was given another battering. The Chinese exploited the weakness of the South Korean units, who broke and ran from the Communists as they had the previous June. Ridgway drove north of Seoul on New Year's Day and found "ROK soldiers by the truckloads" retreating, "without order, without arms, without leaders . . . They had thrown their rifles and pistols away." By January 3, Ridgway had no choice but to order the evacuation of Seoul, the second time in the war it would be lost to the Communists. Inchon, the site of MacArthur's triumphant amphibious landing the previous September, was abandoned on January 5. The Eighth Army fell back to the Kum River, 35 miles south of Seoul. Although no one knew it at the

The Nineteenth Infantry Regiment works its way through the snowy mountains about 10 miles north of Seoul, attempting to locate the enemy lines and positions, on January 3, 1951. *(National Archives/DOD, War & Conflict, #1431)*

time, this would be the farthest south the UN forces would retreat for the remainder of the Korean War.

The Chinese offensive petered out after the first week in January, as their supply lines were stretched too thin. And with every passing week, they faced a more formidable foe. Unlike the retreat from North Korea in December, the Americans were not "bugging out" this time. They retreated in good order and then turned and fought when they reached strong defensive positions. Much of the credit for the change was owed to General Ridgway. He instilled in his men a new aggressiveness. Capturing territory, he told them, was not going to win or lose the war; instead, their goal should be to kill as many of the enemy as possible. Ridgway was soon a familiar figure along the front lines in Korea, famed for grenades he wore strapped on his combat jacket. The trouble with the Eighth Army, he told his officers, was that it had been road-bound; the Chinese had controlled the hills and were pounding U.S. truck convoys at will. U.S. soldiers had to get out of trucks and jeeps and up into the hills on foot, if they wanted to win the war. Army officers who would not lead by example, and take some risks, were sent packing back to the United States. Ridgway himself probably took more risks than was wise for a commanding general. He flew reconnaissance missions in a light observation plane over enemy territory, scouting out the possibilities for offensive action.

Under Ridgway's command, the Eighth Army took other steps to improve the morale of its soldiers. A rest and recuperation (R&R) program was set up, so that soldiers who had spent months on the front line could spend five days' leave enjoying the comforts available in Tokyo. The Mobile Army Surgical Hospitals (MASH), designed to provide high-quality emergency medical care to wounded soldiers, were upgraded. Wounded soldiers, evacuated from the front by helicopter, knew that their chances of survival were good if they could reach a MASH unit. (The MASH units would later become famous, thanks to the 1970 movie and 1970s television show *M*A*S*H*.) And in a war

General Ridgway, succeeding Gen. Walton Walker as U.S. Eighth Army commander, tours Battlefield with General MacArthur (front).
(National Archives)

Personnel of the 8225th Mobile Army Surgical Hospital in Korea
(National Archives)

where sudden surprise attacks were always a danger, and where becoming a prisoner of war could be a fate worse than death, Ridgway promised that units cut off by the enemy would not be abandoned without every possible effort being made to come to their rescue.

Ridgway gave orders for the Eighth Army to resume its offensive on January 25. Against light Chinese resistance, the Eighth Army recaptured much of the territory it had lost earlier in the month, including the port of Inchon. In mid-February the Chinese struck back. The U.S. Army's Twenty-third Regiment and a French battalion fought a bloody battle against the Chinese from February 13 to 15 for control of an area near Chipyong-ni. This was known as the Battle of the Twin Tunnels, for the two railroad tunnels penetrating a nearby mountain. Eighteen thousand Chinese troops besieged the UN defenders. The Twenty-third Regiment's commander, Col. Paul Freeman, would later call it "the most desperate fight that I participated in during my entire time in Korea." His men fought hand to hand with the Chinese for control of the hilltops. As usual, the Chinese saved their most ferocious attacks for nighttime. With flares lighting up the darkness, machine-gunner Pete Schultz recalled, "We could see [the Chinese] tumbling down like bowling

Helicopters in the Korean War

THANKS TO THE POPULARITY OF THE CBS TELEVISION series *M*A*S*H,* which ran from 1972 to 1983, the medical evacuation helicopter came to be one of the most widely recognized visual symbols of the Korean War in American popular memory. Many lives were saved by the innovative use of this new form of aircraft in swiftly transporting the wounded from the battlefront to mobile army surgical hospitals. But helicopters found other path-breaking uses in the war—as reconnaissance aircraft, in air-sea rescue operations, and for troop and supply transport. The marines made the most extensive use of helicopters in nonmedical operations. Marine Helicopter Transport Squadron 161, for example, equipped with 10-seat Sikorsky cargo helicopters, airlifted nearly 1,000 marines to the battlefront in one operation in November 1951, anticipating the much more extensive use of helicopters by both the marines and the U.S. Army in "airmobile" operations during the Vietnam War.

U.S. Marines of the First Marine Division Reconnaissance Company make a helicopter landing to relieve the Republic of Korea Eighth Division on September 20, 1951. *(National Archives)*

pins." At one point in the desperate battle, the French soldiers tied red scarves around their heads and charged the Chinese with fixed bayonets. The Fifth Cavalry broke through to relieve the tired UN fighters on the evening of February 15. The battle was estimated to have cost the Chinese 5,000 casualties. The Eighth Army was proving its mettle.

In Tokyo, General MacArthur grew jealous of Ridgway's successes, especially since they undermined his call for an all-out attack against the Chinese mainland. With his usual gift for showmanship, MacArthur showed up in Korea on February 20, announcing to newspaper reporters, "I have just ordered a resumption of the offensive." In fact, Ridgway had drawn up plans for a new offensive called Operation Killer, scheduled to begin February 21, without any aid from MacArthur. MacArthur's shameless grab for publicity endangered the lives of U.S. soldiers by notifying the Chinese of the impending attack. Operation Killer and both Operation Ripper and Operation Rugged, which followed in March, were nonetheless great successes. The UN forces pushed the Chinese back across the Han River. On March 15, the Chinese abandoned Seoul (the fourth and last time the devastated city would change hands during the war). By early April, UN forces once again held territory north of the 38th parallel.

Despite these reverses, the Chinese were by no means defeated. They had kept their main units a jump ahead of the UN offensive. UN forces were slowed down in their advance by the rain and mud, which came in the spring. And the Chinese had nearly inexhaustible supplies of manpower to draw upon. The Chinese armies regrouped north of the 38th parallel. Reinforcements flowed south across the Yalu. By the spring of 1951 the Communist armies, including both the Chinese and North Koreans, included roughly 700,000 men, arrayed against UN ground forces of only 420,000.

The Chinese massed in the "Iron Triangle," a 50-square-mile plateau surrounded by high mountains north of the 38th parallel. On April 22, they launched their spring offensive with 300,000 troops, the largest attack of the war. The Eighth Army pulled back, as far as 35 miles in some sectors, but UN artillery and air strikes pounded the Chinese attackers, inflicting heavy casualties. Some 4,000 men of the British Twenty-ninth Brigade fought for three days against overwhelming Chinese attacks along the Imjin River north of Seoul. They managed to inflict 11,000 casualties on the attackers, while losing a quarter of their own men as casualties. The fight became known as the Battle of

Gloucester Hill, for the heroic but doomed stand of the 850 men of the Gloucestershire Regiment, who were cut off from the rest of the brigade. Only 169 of the Gloucesters made it back to British lines after the battle ended; the rest were killed or captured.

By the end of April the Chinese offensive ground to a halt. They struck again at the UN forces on May 16, but the myth of Chinese invincibility had ended in Korea. The UN forces had proven time and again that they could take the hardest blows the Chinese could deliver, and then strike back with devastating effect. According to the official U.S. Marine Corps history of the war, after the Chinese offensive in May the Communist soldiers were "scourged with bullets, rockets, and napalm as planes swooped down upon them like hawks scattering chickens." The Chinese suffered more than 100,000 casualties in May. For the first time in the war, whole units of the Chinese army began to throw down their arms and surrender. The United Nations pursued the Chinese into the Iron Triangle, seizing control of the strategically important region in June. But this time the UN forces made no attempt to march to the Yalu. Ridgway had learned from MacArthur's mistakes. The war of movement in Korea was coming to an end. The Korean War, like World War I, was becoming a war of fixed positions, barbed wire, minefields, and deep entrenchments on both sides.

On the home front, Americans were increasingly unsettled and disturbed by the direction the war had taken. Americans were not used to fighting "police actions" for limited objectives, particularly when the fighting took place in distant and little-known areas of the globe. Most Americans were united in opposition to the spread of communism. They wanted to see communist aggression brought to a halt in Korea. There was very little antiwar protest during the Korean War, except by small pacifist groups.

But the war did not inspire anything like the sense of high idealism and enthusiasm so evident on the home front in the early days of World War II. In the midst of the Chinese offensive in December 1950, President Truman made a televised speech to the nation. Warning that "Our homes, our nation, all the things we believe in are in great danger," he declared a state of national emergency. To meet the threat in Korea, the government was going to have to raise taxes, while imposing controls on wages and prices. The U.S. military would double in size to 3.5 million. More U.S. boys would be drafted, and more military reserve units would be activated and sent to Korea. (By the fall of 1950, 50,000 were drafted every month; in June 1951, Truman signed a bill extending the draft for another four years and lowering the draft age to 18.)

So Korea meant higher taxes, government interference in the economy, and lengthening casualty lists of young U.S. soldiers sent to fight the war. And as the war dragged on, with no end in sight, many began to question whether it was worth the price or whether it was being fought the right way. In the first summer of fighting, public opinion polls showed that 75 percent of Americans supported Truman's decision to send U.S. troops to Korea. The U.S. public was thrilled by the landing at Inchon, the breakout from Pusan, and the march to the Yalu. But when the good news turned to bad news in November 1950, support for the war rapidly dwindled. After the Chinese intervened, polls showed that 56 percent of Americans believed that the U.S. had made a mistake getting involved in the war, a percentage that remained more or less constant over the next two years.

As the war declined in popularity, so did Truman's presidency. Truman was being hit from two angles by his Republican opponents: He was blamed for getting the United States involved in the war in the first place and also blamed for not doing enough to win the war, once the United States was involved. Sophisticated theories about "containment" and "limited war" found little favor with the American public, who wanted to "win or get out." Within the Republican Party there were leaders who shared the Truman administration's belief in the importance of global collective security policies against Communist expansion, in Europe as well as in Asia. But there was also a strong right-wing element in the Republican leadership that harbored sentiments very similar to those of pre–World War II isolationists. While militantly anticommunist, these right-wingers were suspicious of any U.S. involvement in Europe. They disapproved of Truman's initiative to create the North Atlantic Treaty Organization (NATO), which committed U.S. troops to the defense of Western Europe against the Soviets. Instead, they saw Asia as the key region in the world where the United States should extend and defend its interests. Right-wing Republicans were also suspicious of the strengthening of the executive branch of the government in foreign-policy decision-making, which had taken place during the administration of Franklin Roosevelt and had continued under his successor, Harry Truman. Truman's decision to involve the United States in Korea without a declaration of war was regarded by these Republicans as usurping the power reserved for Congress by the

Constitution. For all these reasons, and also because an unpopular war was damaging the Democrats' prospects for retaining control of the White House in the 1952 election, Republicans hammered away at the Truman administration's policies in Korea.

One of Truman's harshest critics was the junior senator from Wisconsin, Joseph McCarthy. First elected to the Senate in 1946, McCarthy remained an obscure figure until February 1950 when he made a speech in Wheeling, West Virginia, accusing the U.S. State Department of employing hundreds of "card-carrying" members of the Communist Party. It was the influence of these hidden Communists, McCarthy argued, that had led to the "loss of China" the previous year to Mao Zedong's forces. The charges were unfounded; despite repeated Senate investigations, McCarthy never turned up a single Communist in the State Department or in any significant position in the federal government. And China had gone communist due to the incompetence and corruption of the U.S.-backed government of Chiang Kai-shek, not because of any conspiracy in Washington.

Senator Joseph
McCarthy of Wisconsin
(National Archives)

Nevertheless, McCarthy was able to dominate the newspaper headlines with such attacks, and millions of Americans were persuaded that Communists had indeed infiltrated the Democratic administration and were still influencing policy. The Korean War, which broke out four months after McCarthy's Wheeling speech, lent him further ammunition. Speaking on the Senate floor on June 14, 1951, McCarthy hurled charges of treason against the Truman administration. Just six years after the great victory of World War II, the United States was floundering in the face of the Soviet and Communist threat:

> How can we account for our present situation unless we believe that men high in this Government are concerting to deliver us to disaster? This must be the product of a great conspiracy, a conspiracy on a scale so immense as to dwarf any previous such venture in the history of man. . . The American who has never known defeat in war does not expect to be again sold down the river in Asia. He does not want that kind of betrayal. He has had betrayal enough. He has never failed to fight for his liberties . . . He is fighting tonight, fighting gloriously in a war on a distant American frontier made inglorious by the men he can no longer trust at the head of our affairs.

McCarthyism poisoned the political atmosphere in the United States; it made rational debate nearly impossible. Many Americans who were appalled by McCarthy's charges were reluctant to speak out against him, fearing that they too would be accused of sympathizing with the communists. In the midterm congressional elections in November 1950, the Democrats lost heavily in both House and Senate races. McCarthy, who campaigned in several states on behalf of the Republicans, was personally credited with defeating several incumbent Democratic senators. The political woes of the Democrats were just beginning. When Truman moved to rein in General MacArthur in the spring of 1951, his administration became one of the most unpopular in U.S. history.

In the first six months of the war, MacArthur had repeatedly challenged the authority of the Joint Chiefs of Staff and of President Truman to set military and political policy in the Far East. As long as MacArthur seemed to be winning the war, leaders in Washington swallowed their resentments. But after MacArthur led UN forces to disaster in North Korea, his continued acts of insubordination grew intolerable.

McCarthyism Reevaluated in Light of New Evidence

SENATOR JOSEPH MCCARTHY'S EXPLOSIVE CHARGES OF Communist spying in the federal government bitterly divided Americans during the Korean War. A half-century later, thanks to the release of new documentary sources in both Washington and Moscow, McCarthy's charges have reawakened the interest of historians. The most important of these new sources are the Moscow archives of the KGB (the Soviet foreign intelligence agency) and the materials contained in the VENONA Project files, released in Washington by the U.S. National Security Agency in 1995. VENONA was the code name of a top-secret cold war intelligence project designed to decrypt thousands of elaborately coded telegraphic cables between Moscow and its embassy and consulates in the United States that had been intercepted by the U.S. Army's Signal Intelligence Service during and immediately after World War II.

The new sources offer conclusive proof that Julius Rosenberg, executed in 1953 on espionage charges, did indeed pass U.S. nuclear secrets to the Soviets during World War II. They also strongly suggest that Alger Hiss, a State Department official in the 1930s and 1940s, also was guilty of espionage. Altogether, nearly 300 Americans have been shown to be involved, to varying degrees, in Soviet espionage efforts in the years leading up to and during World War II.

At the same time, VENONA and the Moscow archives discredit McCarthy's charges that in 1950 the federal government was still honeycombed with spies. In a 1951 memorandum uncovered in the Moscow archives, KGB officials acknowledged to their superiors that they, in fact, no longer had any significant sources within the U.S. government: "The most serious drawback in organizing intelligence in the U.S. is . . . the lack of agents in the State Department, intelligence service, counterintelligence service, and other most important U.S. governmental institutions."

All through the winter and spring of 1950–51 MacArthur issued a series of provocative statements, which Secretary of State Dean Acheson referred to as the general's "posterity papers." MacArthur wanted to shift the blame for the debacle in Korea from his own shoulders to those of the Truman administration. MacArthur repeatedly demanded

Paratroopers of the 187th (Regimental Combat Team) descend from C-119 planes south of Munsan, Korea, to cut off retreating enemy units on March 23, 1951. *(National Archives/DOD, War & Conflict, #1428)*

to bomb Manchuria, blockade the Chinese coast, and deploy Chiang Kai-shek's soldiers, insisting that otherwise he could not be held responsible for the consequences. Key Republican leaders and conservative newspapers echoed his demands. The fact of the matter was that by giving MacArthur a free hand in the autumn of 1950, the administration had wound up with a half-million Chinese soldiers bearing down on the UN forces in Korea. Any further widening of the war was likely to bring in the Soviet Union as well, scare off the support of UN allies, and possibly lead to the outbreak of nuclear war.

In December 1950, Truman ordered that all public statements by government and military officials on foreign or military policy had to be cleared by proper authorities in Washington. MacArthur was the clear target of the order. But he would not be silenced and repeatedly ran afoul of the order. Things came to a head at the end of March 1951. On March 14, without consulting anyone, MacArthur issued an ultimatum to the Chinese, threatening them with all-out war if they did not agree to negotiations. He ridiculed their military capability and predicted that "expansion of [UN] military operations to [China's] coastal areas and interior bases" would "doom Red China to the risk of imminent military collapse." At that very moment, as MacArthur well knew, Truman had been preparing another offer to the Chinese for negotiations and a cease-fire. MacArthur's belligerent statement torpedoed any possibility that the Chinese would respond favorably to the president's offer. According to Dean Acheson, Truman learned of the news "in a state of mind that combined disbelief with controlled fury."

The final straw came on April 5, when the Republican minority leader in the House of Representatives, Congressman Joseph W. Martin, read a letter on the floor of Congress that he had received from MacArthur. Martin had earlier written to MacArthur asking if he agreed that Chinese Nationalist troops should be used to open up a second front against the Communists on China's mainland. MacArthur wrote back that Martin's proposal "is in conflict with neither logic nor . . . tradition." And, he concluded, "There is no substitute for victory." In other words, the Truman policy of limited war for limited objectives was mistaken. This would be the last time MacArthur would be allowed to challenge the authority of his commander in chief. On April 11, Truman ordered MacArthur relieved of all his commands. At a White House press conference, reporters were handed a statement bearing a terse message from the president:

> With deep regret I have concluded that General of the Army Douglas MacArthur is unable to give his wholehearted support to the policies of the United States government and of the United Nations in matters pertaining to his official duties . . . I have decided that I must make a change of command in the Far East. I have, therefore, relieved General MacArthur of his commands.

General Ridgway was appointed to MacArthur's post as UN commander, and Gen. James Van Fleet took over command of the Eighth Army. Due to botched scheduling, Truman's message was released to the press before a private message could be sent to MacArthur in Tokyo, where he learned of his relief from a radio broadcast.

Millions of Americans felt that the president had gravely wronged the hero of Bataan and Inchon. Some 100,000 telegrams poured into the White House, most of them critical of the firing. Gallup polls revealed that the public supported MacArthur over Truman by 69 percent to 29 percent. Conservative newspapers called for Truman's impeachment. When Truman showed up to throw out the first pitch at the Washington Senators season-opening baseball game in mid-April, he was booed by the fans. On the other hand, U.S. allies were greatly relieved; in Britain there were cheers in the House of Commons when the news of MacArthur's relief was announced. In Korea, most soldiers just shrugged when they heard the news. Army lieutenant Jim Sheldon remembered: "MacArthur was too distanced from us for his going to make much impact. The only sort of thing we noticed was the food getting better after Ridgway took over."

MacArthur returned home to a hero's welcome, including a ticker tape parade in New York City that attracted more than 7 million spectators. On April 19, he addressed a joint meeting of Congress, in which he repeated his refrain, "In war, indeed, there can be no substitute for victory." The speech attracted the largest viewing audience in the history of television up to that time, and millions of Americans were stirred by MacArthur's conclusion, when he quoted the words of an old army ballad:

"Old soldiers never die; they just fade away." And like the old soldier of that ballad, I now close my military career and just fade away—an old soldier who tried to do his duty as God gave him the light to see that duty. Goodbye.

A bitter debate over MacArthur's dismissal followed in hearings over the next two months before the Senate Armed Services and Foreign Relations committees. While Truman remained personally unpopular, the American public grudgingly swung around to his side in the dispute. Truman had the support of the Joint Chiefs of Staff, who criticized MacArthur's impetuous strategy in Korea. And even if they did not like the current resident in the White House, most Americans continued to believe that civilian leaders had the constitutional right and responsibility to control the policies carried out by military leaders. Talk of running MacArthur as a Republican presidential candidate against Truman in 1952 soon faded away.

For all the fury of political debate during the Korean War over the issues of communist influence in Washington and over MacArthur's

On his first visit to the United States in 14 years, Gen. Douglas MacArthur addresses an audience of 50,000 at Soldier's Field in Chicago, April 1951. *(National Archives)*

dismissal, most Americans lived through the war years virtually untouched by the conflict. Since young men could avoid or at least delay military service through college deferments, the middle class was by and large spared the experience of seeing its sons sent off to war. Economically, Americans of all classes were doing better than they had in years. They took vacations, went to the movies, and took in a ball game as if there were no war at all. (Boston Red Sox fans were torn between pride and dismay when the team's star slugger, Ted Williams, was sent to Korea as a pilot with his Marine Corps reserve unit; after flying 39 combat missions, Williams returned to finish out the 1953 season, batting over .400 in the 37 games he got to play in.) For civilian consumers, there was no need to choose between guns and butter as there had been during World War II. The United States's enormous industrial capacity, and the lack of serious economic competition from war-devastated Europe and Japan, fed a consumer boom of unprecedented proportions. The assembly lines of Detroit turned out both tanks and passenger automobiles all through the Korean War. By 1953, the United States, with 6 percent of the world's population, accounted for about half the world's production of manufactured goods.

After years of economic hard times in the Great Depression of the 1930s, and of the rationing of scarce consumer goods in World War II,

RIDGWAY TAKES COMMAND

Americans were scrambling to make up for lost time in enjoying the good life. They had money to spend. Unemployment, which had stood at close to 5 percent of the workforce in the summer of 1950, dropped to less than 2 percent by 1953. Despite the inflationary pressures brought by the war, real wages (the amount of money the average worker brought home, adjusted to account for the cost of living) continued to climb dramatically during the 1950s. And Americans were encouraged to go into debt, as never before in U.S. history, through such innovations as the credit card.

The great symbol of U.S. prosperity in the 1950s was the television set, a home entertainment device virtually nonexistent at the end of World War II. During the Korean War years, a majority of Americans first acquired their TVs, and by 1954 two-thirds of U.S. families owned at least one television set. But Korea is not remembered as a "television war" in the way that Vietnam would later be. Television news was in its infancy. Camera equipment was bulky and unreliable, and it took several days to get film out of Korea, processed and onto U.S. screens. Most

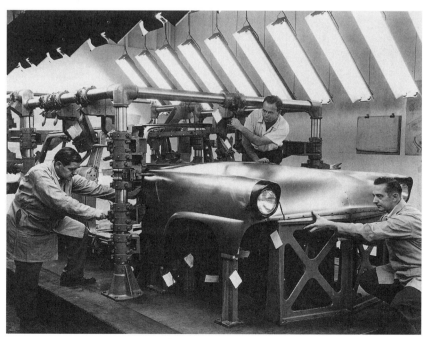

Men working on a Ford automobile assembly line *(Library of Congress)*

U.S. Marines wounded at Kari San Mountain are evacuated via helicopter and flown to a nearby hospital for treatment, May 23, 1951.
(National Archives/DOD, War & Conflict, #1453)

Americans still got their news of the war from the radio, from newspapers, and from weekly photo magazines like *Life*. (The photographs taken by David Douglas Duncan of the marines in "Frozen Chosin" and printed in *Life* stood out for their ability to convey the heroism and tragedy of war.)

But for all the limitations of the medium, television did have an impact. Sitting in their own living rooms, Americans now watched such leaders as Truman and MacArthur deliver speeches that defined the issues of the war. Documentaries about the fighting, particularly those offered by CBS correspondent Edward R. Murrow on his weekly public affairs program *See It Now*, brought at least some of the realities of combat home to Americans. And television helped to bring an end to Senator Joseph McCarthy's political influence when it offered continuous coverage of the "Army-McCarthy" hearings in 1954, sessions that revealed the senator at his blustering, bullying worst.

As the first anniversary of the North Korean invasion of the South rolled around in June 1951, it was evident that neither side could expect to win any dramatic victory in the war. Early that month, the United

States made a quiet diplomatic approach to the Soviets, suggesting that it was time to sit down to negotiations. The Soviets agreed. The Korean War had proven a disaster for the Communists, not just in terms of Kim Il Sung's thwarted ambition to conquer South Korea, but in stiffening Western resolve to resist Communist expansion. Soviet ambassador to the UN Jacob Malik, in a radio speech on June 23, stated that the Soviet Union wanted to see a cease-fire and settlement of the war. Two days later the official *People's Daily* newspaper in Beijing endorsed Malik's statement. On July 1, the North Koreans agreed to armistice talks. And on July 10 UN and Communist negotiators sat down together in truce talks for the first time in the South Korean city of Kaesong. But the war was not over by any means. Two years of hard fighting and heavy casualties still lay ahead.

7

LONG ROAD TO PEACE

Negotiators from the UN Command, led by U.S. Navy vice admiral C. Turner Joy, met for the first time with their counterparts from Communist China and North Korea for truce talks on July 10, 1951. They convened in the Communist-controlled city of Kaesong in western South Korea. Any hopes that these talks would bring the killing to an end quickly were soon dashed. The two sides argued endlessly over such issues as the exchange of prisoners of war and the exact location of the truce demarcation line that would in effect become the new border of North and South Korea. The negotiations were in continuous danger of collapse. The Communists broke off the talks in August 1951. Negotiations were not resumed until October of that year in a new location, the village of Panmunjom in southern North Korea. When no substantial progress had been made by October 1952, the UN negotiators walked out. It was not until April of 1953 that the first real breakthrough was made in negotiating an end to the war. In the meantime, fierce fighting continued on the ground and in the air, hundreds of thousands of soldiers and civilians would lose their lives, and a new administration would take office in Washington with the promise of ending the war.

As the second year of the war began in the summer of 1951, the Eighth Army under command of Gen. James Van Fleet was digging in along a defensive line the Americans called "the Kansas Line." Stretching across the Korean Peninsula, it climbed northeastward from the mouth of the Imjin River south of the 38th parallel, to a point 25 miles north of the 38th parallel on the Korean Peninsula's eastern coast. A more advanced but less heavily fortified line, known as "Wyoming," stretched in an arc above the Kansas Line in the western half of the peninsula. The soldiers and marines sheltered in deep bunkers and trenches, protected by barbed wire and minefields, gave the Eighth Army's positions the appearance of a World War I battlefront. The Chinese and North Koreans built up similar fortifications on their own side of the line.

UN commanders worried that their troops would grow complacent with the start of truce talks. General Van Fleet warned that a "sitdown army" might collapse "at the first sign of an enemy effort." Van Fleet later complained that UN forces missed an opportunity to drive for a decisive victory in 1951. He wanted to launch new amphibious landings in North Korea to outflank the enemy. But the new Far East commander, General Ridgway, was more cautious than his predecessor, Douglas MacArthur, had been. Remembering the disasters of the previous year, Ridgway reined in his aggressive subordinate. In a memo he wrote in May 1951, Ridgway made it clear that future UN offensives would seek only to deliver "advantages in support of . . . diplomatic

One M-46 Patton tank pulls another from the mud on the way to the front, April 1951. *(U.S. Army Military History Institute)*

"Germ Warfare" and Communist Propaganda

BOTH SIDES IN THE KOREAN WAR MADE USE OF psychological warfare techniques designed to undermine the morale of their enemies. The United States used its command of the skies to drop billions of propaganda leaflets over Communist lines urging soldiers to desert, and over North Korean cities seeking to undermine civilian morale. Radio broadcasts and loudspeaker appeals were also used to influence frontline soldiers.

The Communists had fewer resources and virtually no successes when it came to influencing frontline soldiers. Instead, they concentrated on undermining civilian support for the war effort on the home front. They sought to discredit the UN cause by publicizing charges of U.S. atrocities against Korean and Chinese civilians. In 1951 Beijing Radio charged that the United States was using chemical warfare, including "poison gas of an asphyxiating type" dropped from U.S. aircraft and employed against soldiers and civilians. The United States denied the charges, and most accounts of the war accept that they had no merit. In 1952 the Communists launched a new propaganda offensive, this time charging that the United States was conducting "germ warfare." Using coerced confessions from U.S. pilots they had taken prisoner, the Communists charged in the United Nations that U.S. planes were dropping bacterial agents over the North Korean and Chinese countryside. Anthrax, plague, cholera, encephalitis, meningitis, and smallpox, as well as plant and animal diseases, were allegedly being spread by means of diseased insects, spiders, ticks, and rodents.

The United States again vehemently denied the charges. Although the U.S. military was secretly experimenting with biological warfare techniques (helped in this endeavor by captured Japanese officers who had conducted experiments with spreading diseases such as bubonic plague in Manchuria during the war), no credible evidence has been produced that the United States actually employed such methods in the Korean War.

negotiations." The Communists had probably drawn similar conclusions after the failure of their spring offensive. Both sides wanted to keep up pressure on their opponent, but the point of the fighting now was not to deliver a knockout blow. Rather, the UN and the

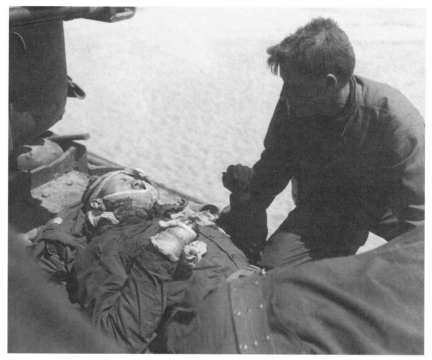

Crew members of Company D, Eighty-ninth Tank Battalion, give first aid to wounded soldier, during action against Chinese Communist forces northeast of Seoul, Korea, May 1, 1951. *(National Archives/DOD, War & Conflict, #1452)*

Communists each attempted to make limited battlefield gains that could then be used as bargaining chips in the armistice negotiations.

Although by the summer of 1951 the Korean War was being fought for limited aims, it still proved extremely costly in human life. In June the United Nations launched a new offensive called Piledriver, pushing north from the Kansas Line. Despite strong Chinese resistance and unfavorable weather, the Eighth Army reached the base of the Communist stronghold in the Iron Triangle region. The anniversary of the North Korean invasion, June 25, saw UN forces controlling a swath of North Korean territory averaging about 10 miles deep, north of the 38th parallel. Operation Piledriver gave the UN control of east-west roads along which the Communists had previously been able to shift troops easily. But Van Fleet was disappointed by the Eighth Army's failure to capture the stubbornly defended Iron Triangle.

The Eighth Army resumed the offensive in mid-August, concentrating on a limited sector of the battlefront east of the Iron Triangle. Van Fleet wanted to keep up pressure on the Communists, while spoiling any plans they had to launch their own offensive. UN and Communist forces battled for control of the hills that rose above a circular valley called the Punchbowl, 15 miles northeast of the Hwachon Reservoir. The North Koreans held the high ground, from which they could direct artillery fire against the UN positions on the Kansas Line. ROK troops led off the assault, followed by the marines of the First Division and soldiers from the Second U.S. Infantry Division. Another hillside that became known as Bloody Ridge was cleared by the Americans, bunker by bunker, with grenades and flamethrowers. By early September Bloody Ridge was in UN hands, at a cost of 2,700 casualties. A monthlong battle followed for control of Heartbreak Ridge, costing the U.S. Second Division 3,700 casualties. That fall, the U.S. First Cavalry also took heavy casualties in fighting near the town of Sangnyong, farther to the west.

In November the Eighth Army offensive ground to a halt. Many weary veterans of the fighting were at last withdrawn from Korea. The First Cavalry, which would suffer four times as many casualties in the 16 months it was in action in the Korean War than it did in all of World War II, was sent back to Japan in December. The Twenty-fourth Infantry Division, the first U.S. military unit to fight in Korea, followed it to Japan in January 1952. There were also several important changes in command in the next year. In May 1952, General Ridgway stepped down as commander in chief of the Far East Command and the United Nations Command to take over the post of NATO commander in Europe. (The previous NATO commander, Gen. Dwight Eisenhower, resigned to run as the Republican candidate for president.) Gen. Mark Clark, who had commanded U.S. troops in Italy during World War II, succeeded Ridgway as Far East and UN commander. And in February 1953, Gen. Maxwell Taylor, commander of the 101st Airborne Division during World War II, succeeded General Van Fleet as commander of the Eighth Army in Korea.

The United Nations would not launch another major offensive in the ground war. The Chinese went on the offensive several times, in the fall of 1952 and the spring of 1953, but their advances were contained without significant loss of territory. While the war receded from the headlines in U.S. newspapers, American lives continued to be lost in small-scale engagements, on patrols and in artillery attacks. (This is the period of the war depicted in the popular television series *M*A*S*H*.) However, one of the fiercest battles of the war came in the waning months of the conflict, when the Chinese attacked the UN-held "Pork Chop Hill" on the eastern side of the Iron Triangle. The U.S. Seventh Infantry Division bore the brunt of the attack in July 1953. The Americans inflicted thousands of casualties on the Communists, but in the end the scarred and useless hill was abandoned to the enemy.

President Truman wanted to contain the Communists in Korea with a minimal expenditure of American lives. That led to a decision in 1951 to step up air operations against the Communists. The U.S. Air Force and naval and Marine Corps fliers provided close air support of ground troops, flying thousands of missions over the battlefront to bomb and strafe enemy troop concentrations and supply lines. These were known as tactical air operations. U.S. airmen also flew strategic bombing missions, designed to weaken the ability of the Communists to continue the war, through attacks on factories, power plants, transportation, and communication systems; they also bombed some civilian population centers in North Korea.

Virtually unopposed over the skies of South Korea, UN airmen faced heavy antiaircraft fire and enemy fighters over North Korea. The Korean War saw the first aerial combat between jet fighters. The U.S. pilots were far more successful in these battles than their Communist opponents. In May 1951, air force captain James Jabara became the world's first jet ace when he added two more kills to the four MiGs he had already shot down. (An "ace" is a fighter pilot who shoots down five enemy planes.) Jabara would shoot down nine more MiGs by the end of the war, for a total of 15. All told, U.S. pilots would down more than 950 enemy aircraft during the war. The United States suffered the loss of 147 aircraft in aerial combat and more than 1,000 other airplanes to ground fire, mechanical failure, or other causes. (Among other pilots who lost their lives was air force captain James A. Van Fleet, Jr., son of the Eighth Army commander, who was shot down over North Korea in April 1952.)

The United Nations launched a major air offensive in May 1952, seeking to break the stalemate in negotiations at Panmunjom. Among the targets they hit were the hydroelectric power stations on the Yalu River. Ninety percent of electrical power capacity was destroyed in two

B-29 Superfortresses from the Far East Air Force's Bomber Command drop their loads on North Korean targets. *(U.S. Army Military History Institute)*

days of attacks. Pyongyang and other North Korean cities were flattened in air attacks. And in the last months of the war, the UN Air Force attacked irrigation dams in North Korea in an effort to destroy the country's rice crop. Despite the massive destruction from the air, there is little evidence that these attacks hastened the end of the war. As had been true in World War II, and would again be proven in Vietnam, bombers were effective when used to support ground troops, but of limited value when used as a strategic weapon.

The fate of prisoners of war (POWs) was one of the most controversial issues of the Korean War and proved a major stumbling block in the Panmunjom negotiations. Atrocities against enemy captives were committed by both sides. The ROKs were notorious for their brutal treatment of both enemy soldiers and of civilians suspected of supporting the communists. And in the heat of battle, U.S. soldiers sometimes ignored the Geneva conventions, the international agreements that are intended to protect POWs. Angered at the loss of friends in battle or

finding prisoners an inconvenient burden, Americans in some
instances shot the North Koreans and Chinese who fell into their
hands. But if the prisoners taken by Americans survived their capture,
their subsequent treatment and chances of survival were relatively
good. That was not the case for those Americans and other UN soldiers
who were captured by the Communists. More than 8,000 Americans
were listed as missing in action during the Korean War. Many of them
were killed in combat and simply unaccounted for in the confusion of
battle. Slightly fewer than 400 Americans are known to have died in
captivity, but there may have been thousands of others whose deaths in
captivity went unrecorded.

The North Koreans became notorious for their brutal treatment of
prisoners after advancing UN forces stumbled on the remains of mass
executions of U.S. soldiers in the early days of the war. Other UN prisoners died of starvation, exposure, or execution on long marches to
the North Korean prison camps near the Yalu River. Philip Deane, a
British journalist captured early in the war, witnessed a terrible scene in
October 1950, as he marched in a column of prisoners to the rear. The

Four North Korean soldiers are taken prisoner. *(National Archives)*

Five former POWs—three Americans and two Australians—warm them-selves after being returned unharmed to the Allied lines by Chinese soldiers. *(Lyndon Baines Johnson Library & Museum)*

English-speaking North Korean officer in charge, called "the Tiger" by the prisoners, had forbidden anyone from dropping out of the line of march. When prisoners continued to fall by the wayside from exhaustion, he announced he would kill one of the U.S. officers, Texas-born army lieutenant Cordus H. Thornton, for disobeying orders. As Deane reported, the Tiger taunted Thornton:

> "That is what would happen in the American Army also, is it not?"
> "In the American Army, sir, there would be a trial."
> The Tiger turned to the assembled Korean soldiers. "I have the authority to kill him. He has disobeyed orders. What must I do?"
> "Kill him," screamed the soldiers, "kill them all."
> "You see," said the major to Lieutenant Thornton, "you have had your trial, a People's Trial, People's Justice. Now I will kill you."
> "In Texas," said Thornton, a tone of contempt in his voice, "we call that lynching, not justice."

LONG ROAD TO PEACE

The major blindfolded Thornton, then shot him in the back of the neck with a pistol. Thornton's body was left in a ditch.

Americans who fell into Chinese hands were somewhat luckier. In the early days of the war, the Chinese actually released some of the Americans they took prisoner after giving them a meal and cigarettes. (The purpose of such generosity was to undermine the morale of U.S. troops, making them more likely to surrender when they learned of Chinese leniency.) The Chinese took thousands of prisoners during their November–December offensive in 1950; many would be held in POW camps along the Yalu River for the next two and a half years. No Americans ever managed to escape from these camps; since there was no neutral or friendly territory nearby for the UN prisoners to escape to, the communists did not even bother putting up fences around their camps. For the most part the prisoners were not beaten or tortured, but food was scarce and medical care virtually nonexistent. As a result, nearly four out of every 10 UN soldiers known to have been taken as

North Korean and Chinese prisoners of war *(National Archives)*

U.S. POWs in the Korean War

IN THE EARLY MONTHS OF THE WAR, U.S. AND OTHER UN prisoners taken by the North Koreans could expect harsh treatment at the hands of their captors, often including the summary execution of the wounded or the sick. Conditions varied from moment to moment, depending on the whim of local North Korean commanders. In one notorious "death march" that took place in November 1950, 130 of the 700 POWs who set off on a 120-mile forced march were killed by North Korean guards before they reached their destination—more than one dead man per mile along the line of the march.

By the spring of 1951 the Chinese had taken custody of all UN prisoners. In some ways conditions improved; the prisoners were held in camps where there was less chance of random executions. But mistreatment took on a more systematic, purposeful character. The Chinese treated the prisoners under their control as a resource to be exploited for propaganda purposes. They used physical and psychological mistreatment to secure both converts and "confessions." The term *brainwashing* came into wide usage during and after the Korean War to describe the manipulation of U.S. prisoners for political ends. Prisoners were divided by nationality, rank, and the degree to which they were regarded as potentially sympathetic. Privileges and punishments were doled out depending on how cooperative an individual prisoner proved. The communists sought to wear down prisoner morale through isolation, anti-UN and anti-American lectures, and other methods. Some prisoners, especially pilots, were singled out for

POWs died in captivity. The Chinese also set about to convert their prisoners through systematic "reeducation." Prisoners were required to sit through endless lectures on the virtues of the communist system and the evils of capitalism and imperialism.

The Chinese proved skillful at breaking down the loyalties and sense of solidarity that had sustained prisoners in earlier wars. The Communists launched an international propaganda campaign in 1952, charging that the United States was dropping bacteria from the air over North Korea to spread disease. U.S. Air Force crewmen came under intense psychological pressure, called brainwashing, to admit that they had been

often brutal interrogations in the hopes of producing statements confessing war crimes.

Of 7,140 U.S. servicemen known to be taken prisoner, at least 2,700 died in captivity.

Recently repatriated in the UN POW exchange, POWs pose for a group photograph with their flight nurses at Tachikawa Air Base, Japan. *(National Archives)*

shot down while engaged in "germ warfare." Several hundred POWs gave in to such pressures, either convinced that the charges were true or hoping to gain better treatment; some made broadcasts or wrote statements for the Communists. After the war, 14 American POWs would be court-martialed by the army for collaborating with the enemy. In the case of 21 Americans, Communist brainwashing proved so effective that at the end of the war they refused repatriation and stayed to live in China.

UN forces captured 170,000 North Korean and Chinese prisoners. Many of them were held on an island off the southeast coast of the Korean Peninsula called Koje-do. The Communists managed to turn the camps into another front in the war against the United Nations. Some Communists deliberately allowed themselves to be captured. They set up resistance organizations among the prisoners. Radios were smuggled into POW compounds, allowing the resistance movement to communicate with communist leaders in North Korea. U.S. and ROK guards controlled the perimeters of the camp, but they could not control what went on inside the compound. When U.S. troops moved into the camp in February 1952 to reassert control, a riot broke out in which 77 prisoners and one U.S. soldier were killed. An international uproar ensued over charges of inhumane treatment of the prisoners. In May, the Communists managed to seize U.S. brigadier general Francis T. Dodd, the camp commander, and held him hostage until the United States agreed to improve conditions in camp. When U.S. troops again moved into the compound to reassert control, the resulting battle cost the lives of 31 POWs and one American. Thousands of spears, knives, and Molotov cocktails (gasoline bombs) were confiscated from the prisoners.

When U.S. troops freed Red Army prisoners from Nazi POW camps in World War II, they discovered that some of them did not want to be sent back to the Soviet Union. Returned against their will, many of the Soviet POWs were shipped to prison camps in Siberia or executed. For humanitarian and political reasons the United States adopted a new policy in the Korean War. No Communist prisoners would be repatriated to the North Koreans or Chinese after the war, unless they agreed to go. Many of the North Korean POWs were former ROK soldiers, who preferred to stay in South Korea; many Chinese POWs were former Nationalists who preferred to go to Taiwan. All told, about 50,000 Communist prisoners refused repatriation. In Panmunjom, the Communists at first demanded the return of all their POWs, charging that those refusing repatriation had been pressured to do so by their UN captors. Later, the Communists would accept the principle of voluntary repatriation, but only if the prisoners' refusals to return to their homelands were verified by officials from a neutral country. Haggling over the details of the repatriation process took up months of negotiations at Panmunjom, while the war dragged on.

The unending bloodletting in Korea proved a major issue in the 1952 U.S. presidential campaign. The Republicans, long out of office and hungry for a victory, sought to capitalize on the public's growing war weariness. President Truman's standing in public opinion polls dropped to record low levels, and in March 1952 he announced that he

President-elect Dwight D. Eisenhower talks with men of the Third U.S.
Infantry Division on December 4, 1952, south of Chorwon. *(Lyndon Baines
Johnson Library & Museum)*

would not run for reelection. The Democrats nominated Illinois governor Adlai Stevenson in his place. Although Stevenson proved an attrac-
tive candidate, he faced a formidable foe in Dwight David Eisenhower.
Eisenhower, popularly known as "Ike," had been commander of Allied
forces in the European theater of war during World War II. Eisenhower's name was bound up with proud memories of the simpler, more
clear-cut conflict of the 1940s, when, as MacArthur liked to say, there
had been "no substitute for victory." The Republicans hit hard at the
Democrats for supposedly allowing Communists to infiltrate the government and influence foreign policy. Eisenhower did not promise victory in Korea. What he did promise, in a nationally televised speech in
October 1952, was that, if elected, he would go to Korea for a firsthand
look at the situation. "Only in that way," he declared, "could I learn how
best to serve the American people in the cause of peace."

Eisenhower's promise was a brilliant campaign gambit, appealing, at
the same time, to those who hoped for an increased military effort in
Korea for victory and to those who hoped for an end to the conflict

through negotiated settlement. In November 1952, Ike was elected president by a comfortable margin, ending 20 years of Democratic control of the White House. And in December, as U.S. troops prepared to observe their third Christmas in Korea, Ike made good on his campaign promise and visited the battlefront. The trip was a public relations success, convincing the American people that they once again had a decisive leader in charge in Washington. But in reality Eisenhower's brief visit had little effect on the conduct of either the war or the negotiations.

The new administration did not have any better idea of how to end the war than its discredited Democratic predecessor. Eisenhower and his secretary of state, John Foster Dulles, engaged in some atomic "saber rattling." Eisenhower's military advisers considered the use of atomic weapons to break the stalemate, but in the end the president took no steps toward employing them. How seriously the Communists took the threat of nuclear attack remains unknown. The administration did step

Rear Adm. John C. Daniel waves signed document authorizing the exchange of sick and wounded, April 1953, Panmunjom.
(National Archives)

up the scale and intensity of air attacks on North Korea, and that may have had some impact on the Communists' decision to negotiate.

The real breakthrough came in March 1953 after Soviet leader Joseph Stalin died of illness in Moscow. His successors were eager to end the war. On March 28, the Communists indicated willingness to accept an earlier UN proposal for the exchange of sick and wounded prisoners of war. Chinese foreign minister Zhou Enlai announced that his government was willing to reconsider the whole issue of the repatriation of prisoners of war that had led to the impasse in negotiations at Panmunjom. At the end of April, in Operation Little Switch, the communists handed over 684 sick or wounded UN prisoners (including 149 Americans) in exchange for 6,670 sick or wounded communist prisoners held by the United Nations. At the same time negotiations in Panmunjom, which had been suspended since the previous October, resumed. Finally, at the start of June, the communists announced their willingness to accept the principle of no forcible repatriation of unwilling prisoners of war.

A last-minute roadblock to the settlement of the war was thrown up by Syngman Rhee. The South Korean leader still clung to his dream of marching north and reunifying all of Korea. He threatened to withdraw ROK forces from UN control and invade the North on his own. Rhee's threat was mostly bombast. Without U.S. backing, the ROK forces were in no position to take on the Communists, as the Chinese proved in late June when they launched a surprise attack on ROK units near Kumsong, obliterating a ROK division. But Rhee had other weapons at his command. He ordered ROK soldiers to open the gates of the POW camps they controlled. Before the Americans were able to reassert control, 25,000 nonrepatriated prisoners, who were supposed to have been turned over to the custody of a neutral nation commission, simply walked out the gates and blended into the local population.

The Communists walked out of the Panmunjom negotiations in outrage. U.S. officials considered overthrowing Rhee's government, if he continued his sabotage of the peace settlement. In the end, Rhee conceded the inevitable. The Communists returned to the truce table. At 10 A.M. on July 27, 1953, the armistice agreement was signed by Maj. Gen. William K. Harrison, representing the UN forces, and Lt. Gen. Nam Il of the North Korean army. Even then, men continued to die for another 12 hours in artillery barrages, until the truce went into effect at 10 P.M.

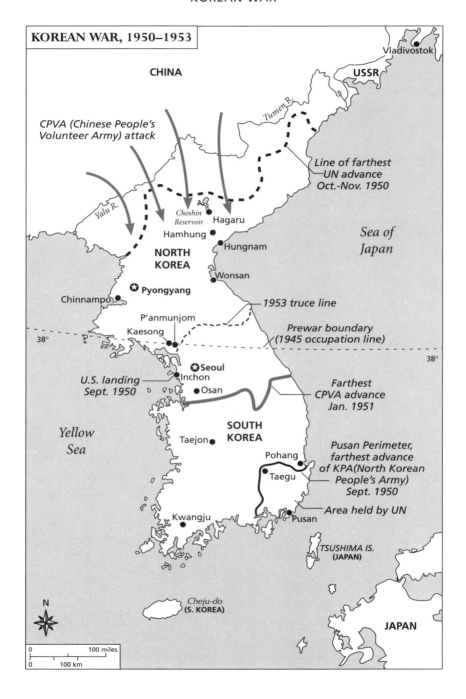

KOREAN WAR, 1950–1953

Vladivostok

CHINA

USSR

CPVA (Chinese People's Volunteer Army) attack

Tumen R.

Line of farthest UN advance Oct.-Nov. 1950

Yalu R.

Choshin Reservoir Hagaru

Hamhung

NORTH KOREA

Hungnam

Sea of Japan

Wonsan

Pyongyang

Chinnampo

1953 truce line

P'anmunjom

Kaesong

38°

Prewar boundary (1945 occupation line)

38°

Seoul

Inchon

U.S. landing Sept. 1950

Osan

Farthest CPVA advance Jan. 1951

Yellow Sea

SOUTH KOREA

Taejon

Pusan Perimeter, farthest advance of KPA(North Korean People's Army) Sept. 1950

Pohang

Taegu

Area held by UN

Kwangju

Pusan

TSUSHIMA IS. (JAPAN)

N

Cheju-do (S. KOREA)

JAPAN

0   100 miles

0   100 km

LONG ROAD TO PEACE

Col. James Murray, Jr., U.S. Marine Corps, and Col. Chang Chun San of the North Korean Communist Army initial maps showing the north and south boundaries of the demarcation zone during the Panmunjom cease-fire talks. *(National Archives)*

The Korean War was over, three years and a little more than a month after it had begun. The last two years of fighting in Korea, while the negotiators dickered at Kaesong and Panmunjom, had cost the U.S. more than 63,000 casualties, including 12,300 men killed in action.

8

LESSONS FROM A
FORGOTTEN WAR

The war in Korea was over. Korea, "Land of the Morning Calm," was in ruins. No one knows exactly how many people died in the war. Total U.S. casualties for the war were 54,246 dead (of whom 33,629 died on the battlefield, the rest of wounds, accidents, or other causes) and 103,284 wounded. ROK Armed Forces lost 59,000 killed. The Chinese and North Koreans lost an estimated half-million soldiers killed in action. Civilian deaths in South and North Korea may have topped 2 million.

All wars bring human suffering, but seldom have so many suffered to gain so little. At the end of the war, the border between North and South Korea was reestablished, along roughly the same line where it had been in June 1950. The Communist leader Kim Il Sung remained in power in North Korea, and the anticommunist leader Syngman Rhee remained in power in South Korea. True, South Korea had been saved from Communist domination, and the United Nations had acted collectively to deter aggression; but no precedent was set in international relations. It would be 40 years before the UN Security Council would again agree to intervene militarily to roll back an act of aggression—by Iraq against Kuwait.

In determining responsibility for the war and its suffering, the greatest portion of blame must fall on Kim Il Sung for ordering the invasion of South Korea. Even though the Korean War was not, as believed at that time in Washington, the opening maneuver of a well-thought-out conspiracy by Joseph Stalin to conquer the West, the Soviet dictator was

U.S. Media and the Korean War

AS HAD BEEN THE CASE IN WORLD WAR II, AMERICANS got most of their news about the Korean War from newspapers and magazines. Television was still in its infancy, and newsreel films took days to reach movie theaters in the United States. Also, as in World War II, and unlike Vietnam, relations between journalists and the military were marked by a high level of cooperation. Few U.S. reporters sent to cover the war doubted the justice of the United Nations cause, and they willingly accepted military censorship of their dispatches in the name of protecting the security of U.S. troops. David Douglas Duncan's photographs and reporting for *Life* magazine, reprinted in the 1951 book *This Is War,* set a high standard for gritty realistic journalism. The frontline reporting of the invasion of Inchon and the retreat from Hungnam by Marguerite Higgins, a reporter for a New York City newspaper, cleared the way for later generations of female war correspondents. As always, reporting on war was a dangerous business: 10 American war correspondents were killed, and one American photographer was captured by the Chinese and spent two and half years in a prisoner-of-war camp.

guilty of giving the North Koreans the go-ahead to pursue their irresponsible adventure. As for the Chinese Communists, they cannot be held responsible for the early phase of the war: They played a minor role in North Korea's decision to go to war, and they provided the West with ample warning of their intention to intervene in the conflict if hostile forces approached the Yalu River. But if the Chinese had halted their advance in January 1951, when they drove UN forces out of North Korea, they might possibly have shortened the war by years.

The United States can be faulted for its willingness to tolerate the undemocratic excesses of Syngman Rhee's government in the years leading up to the North Korean invasion. As was the case in many other regions of the world, in South Korea, U.S. policy makers proved blind to any consideration other than the degree of anticommunism displayed by the regime in power. But recognizing that Rhee's government was a dictatorship does not mean that Kim Il Sung invaded South Korea because he wanted to bring its people democratic liberties. The North Korean dictatorship was far more efficient and ruthless in suppressing democratic dissent than Syngman Rhee ever dreamed of. In an imperfect world, presented with a difficult and dangerous situation in 1950, President Truman acted responsibly in his decision to intervene and in seeking UN sanction for his intervention.

Much less defensible is the amount of leeway he permitted his commander in the region, General MacArthur, in shaping U.S. policy. The war could have been brought to a successful close almost three years earlier, had Truman displayed the wisdom and political courage to halt the UN advance at the 38th parallel, heeding Chinese warnings and ignoring MacArthur's reckless promises of glorious victories to come. A decision to end the war in September 1950 could have saved the lives of hundreds of thousands of Asians and tens of thousands of Americans. It might, conceivably, have saved the Truman presidency from disgrace and the Democrats from political defeat in 1952.

The Korean War left the Korean people more divided than ever. Political change was slow in coming to the troubled Korean Peninsula. Syngman Rhee continued his dictatorial rule in the South until he was overthrown in a student-inspired uprising in 1960. Despite political reforms in the 1980s, South Korea had still not shaken off the legacy of authoritarian rule. In the North, Kim Il Sung remained in power for more than 40 years after the start of the Korean War, making him one of the most durable rulers of the 20th century. Only with the onset of democratic change in the Soviet Union, the collapse of communism in Eastern Europe, and the waning of the cold war at the start of the 1990s did the winds of change begin to be felt in North Korea. Talk of peaceful reunification between North and South Korea was heard both in Seoul and in Pyongyang. North Korea made a small but significant gesture of diplomatic reconciliation to the United States in 1991, returning the remains of 11 U.S. servicemen, among the more than 8,000 Americans still missing from the Korean War.

In the years after the Korean War, memories of the conflict faded in the United States. It has been called "America's forgotten war" and the "unknown war." It ended in an inconclusive stalemate, and there were no great victory celebrations to mark the return of the troops from the fighting.

Yet for a war so quickly forgotten once it was over, the Korean War had a major impact on the United States. It was the decisive moment in the United States's emergence as a world power, one prepared to intervene militarily around the globe in defense of its perceived interests.

LESSONS FROM A FORGOTTEN WAR

The U.S. military establishment, cut to the bone in the aftermath of World War II, would from now on be lavishly funded by Congress. President Eisenhower, who tried to rein in defense spending during his own years in the White House, would warn in his farewell address to the nation in 1960 of the power now wielded by the "military-industrial complex" in U.S. politics. At the same time, the war revealed how a president who chose to could exert broad undefined power. Eisenhower himself had no hesitation in making use of the newly expanded power of the president to shift U.S. troops around the globe without consulting Congress, as he did in 1958 when he sent the marines into Lebanon to prevent a Syrian takeover.

U.S.-Soviet relations began to thaw in the aftermath of the Korean War. Although there were tense confrontations during the next decade over questions such as the status of Berlin and the presence of Soviet missiles in Cuba, the danger of another world war seemed to lessen. The focus of U.S.-Soviet confrontation shifted during the Korean War from Europe to what was beginning to be called the "Third World," the formerly colonized and "underdeveloped" countries of Asia, Africa, and Latin America.

The lessons of the Korean War for U.S. political and military leaders were ambiguous. On the one hand, the war seemed to prove that, through a determined use of U.S. power, communist takeovers of small Third World countries could be prevented. On the other hand, the sobering memory of the Chinese Communist onslaught in the winter of 1950 was a strong argument against getting involved in future ground wars on the Asian continent. In the years after the Vietnam War, U.S. presidents would complain that their hands were tied in foreign policy by a "Vietnam syndrome," a fear of the possibly disastrous consequences of U.S. military involvement. But before there was a Vietnam syndrome there was a Korea syndrome. Assistant Secretary of Defense John MacNaughton sent a memo, entitled "Plan for Action for South Vietnam," in March 1965 to Secretary of Defense Robert McNamara, declaring that "Large U.S. troop deployments [in Vietnam] . . . are blocked by 'French-defeat' and 'Korea' syndromes." To counter this "Korea syndrome," John F. Kennedy had encouraged the U.S. military to develop counterinsurgency tactics to come to the aid of embattled anticommunist nations. Instead of sending in large numbers of U.S. troops, U.S. advisers such as the army's Green Berets would train the soldiers of friendly governments to defend themselves against

The Two Koreas a Half-Century after the Korean War

THE COLD WAR DIVIDED THE WORLD INTO HOSTILE camps. It also divided three nations—Germany, Vietnam, and Korea—into hostile sections aligned with one or the other of the cold war superpowers. Eventually two of the three divided nations were reunited—Vietnam in 1975 under communist leadership, Germany in 1990 under noncommunist leadership. How long will it be until the two Koreas become one again?

In 2001 South Korea had a population of 48 million people, compared to North Korea's 22 million. South Korea is one of the most prosperous nations in Asia, with a strong modern industrial base allowing it to be a major exporter of steel, automobiles, and other manufactured goods. Its annual gross domestic product in 2001 stood at about 765 billion dollars. North Korea, in contrast, is one of the poorest nations in Asia and the world. After years of economic mismanagement, its industrial base is near collapse, and without international humanitarian aid, North Korea would be unable to keep its population from starvation. In 2001 its estimated annual gross domestic product stood at just 22 billion dollars.

Under the leadership of Kim Jong Il, who succeeded his father, Kim Il Sung, as head of the North Korean government in 1994, North Korea has made some effort to reach out from its status as international pariah. In June 2000, Kim Jong Il and South Korea's president Kim Dae Jung met in the first ever south-north summit meeting. Steps toward reconciliation were set back the following year, as U.S. attitudes toward North Korea hardened in the aftermath of the 2001 World Trade Center attack. U.S. president George W. Bush denounced the country as part of an "axis of evil" that included Iran and Iraq. The future of the two Koreas remains an open question.

Communist-led guerrilla uprisings. Among the architects of this new strategy was Gen. Maxwell Taylor, the last commander to lead the Eighth Army during the Korean War.

When counterinsurgency failed to turn back the Communists in Vietnam, the U.S. military reverted to the conventional warfare tactics it had employed in Korea. Units bloodied in Korea, such as the First

LESSONS FROM A FORGOTTEN WAR

A little Korean girl places a wreath of flowers on the grave of a U.S. soldier, while Pfc. Chester Painter and Cpl. Harry May present arms, at the UN cemetery in Pusan. *(National Archives)*

Cavalry (now retrained and equipped as helicopter-borne "Air Cavalry") and the First Marines, were deployed in Vietnam in the summer of 1965. They were under the command of Gen. William C. Westmoreland, who had served in Korea as commander of the 187th Airborne Infantry Regimental Combat Team. With his "search and destroy" tactics, Westmoreland tried to repeat the successful formula used by the Eighth Army in turning back the Chinese offensives in the spring of 1951: When the enemy was out in the open, pour on U.S. firepower. But in Vietnam, despite the awesome technological edge possessed by the United States, the advantages lay with the Communists. Unlike the barren Korean hills, in Vietnam triple-canopy jungle and heavy forests sheltered enemy movements. In South Korea, the civilian population had for the most part opposed the North Korean invasion. In South Vietnam, the Communists succeeded in tapping deeply held nationalist sentiments. Guerrilla stealth, mobility, and popular support could not be countered by helicopter gunships and B-52 strikes.

The real lesson of the Korean War was one of understanding the necessity for prudent limits in the commitment of U.S. military power abroad. In the summer of 1950 the U.S. military was used effectively, even brilliantly as at Inchon, in rolling back an open act of aggression by a foreign invader using conventional tactics. Tempted by the prospects of a glorious march to the Yalu in the fall of 1950, military leaders squandered the victory they had already won. The great military hero of the Korean War was not the vainglorious MacArthur, but the shrewd and careful Gen. Matthew Ridgway. It was Ridgway who, in the words of Korean War veteran and historian Roy Appleman, "redeemed the military honor of the United States in the eyes of the world" when he took over command of the Eighth Army in the dark winter of 1950–51. And it was Ridgway who would warn prophetically, in the spring of 1954, against U.S. military involvement in Vietnam, saying that it would take a half-million men to intervene effectively, and even then the results would be uncertain.

At dawn on July 5, 1950, 1st Lt. William Wyrick was a platoon leader with Task Force Smith, facing the onslaught of North Korean tanks on the highway near Osan. His platoon sergeant, he later recalled, got on the field telephone and called back to unit headquarters for supporting fire from 60 mm mortars. "They won't reach that far," the sergeant was told.

"Well, how about the 81-mm mortars?"
"They didn't come over with us."
"How about the 4.2s [mortars]?"
"The 4.2s can't fire."
"How about the artillery?"
"No communications."
"What about the Air Force?"
"They don't know where we are."
"Call the Navy."
"They can't reach this far."

"Well, then," the sergeant shouted in understandable exasperation, "send me a camera. I want to take a picture of this." It was a moment worth a photograph, in a war worth remembering.

Glossary

aggression Hostile action or assault initiated by one country against another.

airborne People or material delivered by transport planes, helicopters, or other aircraft. An "airborne" unit is specially trained to land with parachutes and will usually do so.

ammunition The materials used in discharging firearms or any weapon that throws projectiles, including powder, shot, shrapnel, bullets, cartridges, and the means of igniting and exploding them, such as primers and fuses. Chemicals, bombs, grenades, mines, and missiles may also be regarded as ammunition.

amphibious warfare The delivery of armed forces from shipboard to a hostile shoreline.

appeasement The act of acceding to the belligerent demands of a group or country, usually involving a sacrifice of principle or justice.

armistice A truce or agreement by warring parties to cease hostilities, at least temporarily but usually with the intention of negotiating a permanent peace. The best known armistice of modern times is the one signed by the Allies and Central Powers that brought World War I to an end at 11 A.M. on November 11, 1918.

atrocity In wartime, an extreme and criminal act carried out by civilians or members of a military unit such as the murder of unarmed civilians.

attrition The wearing down of enemy resources and ability to continue armed conflict, as when military attacks are launched not primarily to take ground but to kill as many of enemy troops as possible.

bazooka A cylindrical rocket launcher carried by infantry in World War II. It fired a projectile intended to penetrate the armor plating of a tank or other military vehicle. Its name was based on its supposed resemblance to a crude musical instrument used by an American comedian of that time, Bob Burns.

beachhead   The area that is the first objective of a military force landing on an enemy shore.

brainwashing   A prolonged psychological process designed to erase an individual's past beliefs and concepts and to substitute new ones.

casualties   Losses of military personnel to enemy action, as killed, wounded, captured, or missing in action.

cease-fire   A suspension of active hostilities between warring parties.

civil war   A war between parties, regions, or ethnic groups within a single country.

coalition   A combination or alliance arranged on a temporary basis, as among wartime allies.

collective security   A policy or principle in international affairs, according to which many countries band together to guarantee the security of individual countries against foreign aggression.

colonialism   A system under which one people or territory are ruled from afar by another country.

communism   The theory and system of social organization that is based on common or state ownership of industry, agriculture, and all other economic enterprises; a system of government based upon the dictatorship of the Communist Party.

convoy   A group of ships or land vehicles traveling together for mutual protection, sometimes under armed escort.

counterinsurgency   The strategy designed to suppress uprisings or insurgencies before they become full-scale wars, it emphasizes mobility and surprise by small units of highly trained specialists. This became the guiding doctrine of U.S. military and political involvement in South Vietnam in the early 1960s.

covert   Undercover or secret; usually used in reference to military actions that involve special operations forces.

draft   A form of involuntary military recruitment through the selection of individuals from the civilian population to join a nation's armed forces. Also known as "conscription."

exile   Enforced or voluntary removal from one's native country.

friendly fire   Combat deaths or wounds caused by the guns, bombs, or artillery of one's own side in a war.

garrison   A permanent military post, or the troops assigned to such a post.

guerrilla warfare   A strategy of warfare in which small bands of civilians or nonuniformed soldiers harass a larger and better-armed enemy through surprise raids or attacks on supply and communication lines, usually depending on the sympathy of local civilians for information and shelter.

howitzer   An artillery piece that delivers shells against a target via a high trajectory.

infiltration   A method of attack in which small units of troops penetrate enemy lines through weak or unguarded points.

inflation   An uncontrollable rise in the amount of currency circulating in an economy, resulting in an undesirable rise in prices for goods and services.

isolationism   A policy of nonparticipation in international affairs.

logistics   The branch of military science concerned with the transportation and supply of troops in the field.

machine gun   A weapon able to deliver a rapid and continuous fire of bullets until the weapon's magazine or firing belt is depleted.

MASH (mobile army surgical hospital)   Field hospitals set up close to frontline military units, to provide immediate surgical care to severely wounded soldiers.

MIA (missing in action)   Military personnel who are unaccounted for after a combat engagement, who may have been killed, captured, or are simply lost, but whose fate remains unknown.

mine   A device containing an explosive charge, buried or placed in a camouflaged setting and designed to explode and kill enemy soldiers or destroy enemy vehicles when they are in its immediate vicinity.

missionaries   Religious believers, sometimes but not always members of the clergy, who travel to distant lands to convert others to their religion.

M-1 rifle   A semiautomatic rifle with an eight-round clip, the M-1 was the standard U.S. infantry rifle in both World War II and the Korean War.

mortar   A small, portable artillery piece that throws shells at high angles onto its target.

napalm   A jellied gasoline incendiary weapon. Dropped from aircraft in canisters or fired from flame-throwers, it burns with fierce heat.

nationalism   Devotion to the interests of one's own nation, including the desire for national independence.

neutrality   The status of a nation that does not participate in a war between other nations.

occupation   The invasion, conquest, and control of a nation or territory by a hostile military force.

pacifist   An opponent of all wars on the principle of opposition to killing.

perimeter   The boundary enclosing a designated area.

POW (prisoner of war)   Military personnel captured and held by the enemy.

propaganda   News and commentary on news released by a government in wartime, intended to persuade domestic and foreign audiences of the righteousness of the government's cause in the war.

quartermaster   A military officer charged with providing shelter, clothing, provisions, fuel, and other materials to troops in the field.

rear echelon   That part of a military force in the field that does not serve in combat in the front lines but rather provides command structure, services, and material to the soldiers at the front.

recoilless rifle   An infantry antitank weapon, developed in the closing days of World War II and employed in the early days of the Korean War. It proved relatively useless in combat against tanks but continued to be used as an antipersonnel weapon.

reconnaissance   A search made for useful military information in the field by means of observation of enemy positions and movements and the physical landscape upon which battles are likely to occur.

reprisal   The infliction of injury on an enemy in warfare in retaliation for an injury suffered at the enemy's hands.

rocket launcher   The 3.5-inch rocket launcher, introduced as a U.S. antitank weapon during the Korean War, proved a distinct improvement over the World War II bazookas with which U.S. troops first tried, ineffectively, to halt North Korean tanks.

sortie   The flight of an aircraft on a single combat mission.

strafe   To attack ground troops or installations from the air with machine-gun fire.

supply depot   A place where a large quantity of military materials, including ammunition, fuel, or food, is gathered prior to distribution to soldiers in the field.

Further Reading

NONFICTION

Alexander, Bevan. *Korea: The First War We Lost.* New York: Hippocrene, 1986.

Appleman, Roy. *Disaster in Korea: The Chinese Confront MacArthur.* College Station: Texas A&M University Press, 1989.

———. *East of Chosin: Entrapment and Breakout in Korea.* College Station: Texas A&M University Press, 1987.

———. *Escaping the Trap: The U.S. Army in Northeast Korea, 1950.* College Station: Texas A&M University Press, 1987.

———. *Ridgway Duels for Korea.* College Station: Texas A&M University Press, 1990.

Blair, Clay. *The Forgotten War: America in Korea, 1950–1953.* New York: Times Books, 1987.

Breuer, William B. *Shadow Warriors: The Covert War in Korea.* New York: John Wiley, 1996.

Bussey, Charles M. *Firefight at Yechon: Courage and Racism in the Korean War.* New York: Macmillan, 1991.

Carew, Tim. *Korea: The Commonwealth at War.* London: Cassell, 1967.

Cotton, James, and Ian Neary. *The Korean War as History.* Atlantic Highlands, N.J.: Humanities Press, 1989.

Cumings, Bruce. *Child of Conflict: The Korean-American Relationship, 1943–1953.* Seattle: University of Washington Press, 1983.

———. *Korea's Place in the Sun: A Modern History.* New York: W. W. Norton, 1997.

———. *The Origins of the Korean War.* Vol. 1, *Liberation and the Emergence of Separate Regimes, 1945–1974.* Princeton, N.J.: Princeton University Press, 1981.

———. *The Origins of the Korean War.* Vol. 2, *The Roaring of the Cataract, 1947–1950.* Princeton, N.J.: Princeton University Press, 1990.

Dae-Sook, Suh. *Kim Il Sung: The North Korean Leader.* New York: Columbia University Press, 1988.

FURTHER READING

Deane, Philip. *I Was a Captive in Korea.* New York: W. W. Norton, 1953.

Dobbs, Charles M. *The Unwanted Symbol: American Foreign Policy, the Cold War, and Korea, 1945–1950.* Kent, Ohio: Kent State University Press, 1981.

Duncan, David Douglas. *This Is War.* New York: Harper and Brothers, 1951.

Evanhoe, Ed. *Darkmoon: Eighth Army Special Operations in the Korean War.* Annapolis, Md.: Naval Institute Press, 1995.

Farrar-Hockley, Sir Anthony. *The British Part in the Korean War.* Vol. 1, *A Distant Obligation.* London: HMSO, 1990.

———. *The British Part in the Korean War.* Vol. 2, *An Honourable Discharge.* London: HMSO, 1994.

Fehrenbach, T. R. *This Kind of War: A Study of Unpreparedness.* New York: Macmillan, 1963.

Foot, Rosemary. *A Substitute for Victory: The Politics of Peacemaking at the Korean Armistice Talks.* Ithaca, N.Y.: Cornell University Press, 1990.

———. *The Wrong War: American Policy and the Dimensions of the Korean Conflict.* Ithaca, N.Y.: Cornell University Press, 1985.

Goncharov, Sergei N., John W. Lewis, and Xue Litai. *Uncertain Partners: Stalin, Mao and the Korean War.* Stanford, Calif.: Stanford University Press, 1993.

Goulden, Joseph. *Korea: The Untold Story.* New York: Times Books, 1982.

Grey, Jeffrey. *The Commonwealth Armies and the Korean War.* Manchester, England: Manchester University Press, 1988.

Halliday, Jon, and Bruce Cumings. *The Unknown War: Korea.* New York: Pantheon, 1988.

Hastings, Max. *The Korean War.* New York: Simon and Schuster, 1987.

Heinl, Robert D. *Victory at High Tide: The Inchon-Seoul Campaign.* Philadelphia: Lippincott, 1968.

James, D. Clayton. *The Years of MacArthur: Triumph and Disaster, 1945–1964.* Boston: Houghton Mifflin, 1985.

Jian, Chen. *China's Road to the Korean War: The Making of the Sino-American Confrontation.* New York: Columbia University Press, 1994.

Kaufman, Burton I. *The Korean War: Challenges in Crisis, Credibility, and Command.* Philadelphia: Temple University Press, 1986.

Knox, Donald. *The Korean War: An Oral History.* Vol. 1, *Pusan to Chosin.* New York: Harcourt, Brace, Jovanovich, 1985.

———. *The Korean War: An Oral History.* Vol. 2, *Uncertain Victory.* New York: Harcourt, Brace, Jovanovich, 1988.

Leckie, Robert. *Conflict: The History of the Korean War.* New York: Putnam, 1962.

MacDonald, Callum A. *Korea: The War before Vietnam.* New York: Free Press, 1986.

Malcolm, Ben S. *White Tigers: My Secret War in North Korea.* Washington, D.C.: Brassey's, 1996.

Marshall, S. L. A. *Pork Chop Hill.* New York: Morrow, 1956.

McCullough, David. *Truman.* New York: Simon and Schuster, 1992.

Merrill, James. *Korea: The Peninsular Origins of the War.* Newark: University of Delaware Press, 1989.

Rees, David. *Korea: The Limited War.* London: Macmillan, 1964.

Ridgway, Matthew B. *The Korean War.* Garden City, N.Y.: Doubleday, 1967.

Shugang, Zhang. *Mao's Military Romanticism: China and the Korean War, 1950–1953.* Lawrence: University Press of Kansas, 1995.

Spanier, John W. *The Truman-MacArthur Controversy and the Korean War.* Cambridge, Mass.: Belknap Press, 1959.

Stanton, Shelby. *America's Tenth Legion: X Corps in Korea, 1950.* Novato, Calif.: Presidio Press, 1989.

Stone, I. F. *The Hidden History of the Korean War, 1950–1951.* Boston: Little, Brown, 1952.

Stueck, William J. *The Korean War: An International History.* Princeton, N.J.: Princeton University Press, 1995.

Summers, Harry G. *Korean War Almanac.* New York: Facts On File, 1990.

Toland, John. *In Mortal Combat: Korea, 1950–1953.* New York: Morrow, 1991.

Van Ree, Eric. *Socialism in One Zone: Stalin's Policy in Korea, 1945–1947.* New York: Oxford University Press, 1988.

Wells, Anne Sharp. *Refighting the Last War: Command and Crises in Korea, 1950–1953.* New York: Free Press, 1993.

Wood, Herbert Fairlie. *Strange Battleground: The Official History of the Canadian Army in Korea.* Ottawa, Ont.: Queen's Printer, 1966.

FICTION

Ahn Jung-hyo. *Silver Stallion: A Novel of Korea.* New York: Soho Press, 1990.

Brady, James. *The Marines of Autumn: A Novel About the Korean War.* New York: St. Martin's, 2001.

Hooker, Richard D. *MASH.* New York: William Morrow, 1997.

Michener, James. *The Bridges at Toko-Ri.* New York: Random House, 1953.

Morris, Willie. *Taps: A Novel.* Boston: Houghton Mifflin, 2001.

Salter, James. *The Hunters.* New York: Vintage Books, 1999.

Simmons, Edwin Howard. *Dog Company Six.* Annapolis, Md.: Naval Institute Press, 2000.

WEBSITES

Korean War History Gallery. Available online. URL: http://www.wpafb.af.mil/museum/history/korea/korea.htm. Downloaded on May 6, 2002.

The Korean War, June 1950–July 1953. Available online. URL: http://www.defenselink.mil/specials/koreanwar/. Downloaded on May 6, 2002.

Index

Page numbers in *italics* indicate a photograph. Page numbers followed by *m* indicate maps. Page numbers followed by *g* indicate glossary entries. Page numbers in **boldface** indicate box features.

INDEX

INDEX

INDEX

INDEX